being caribou

being caribou

five months on foot with an arctic herd

karsten heuer

MILKWEED EDITIONS

Published 2008 by Milkweed Editions

Original hardcover publication 2005 by Mountaineers Books

Printed in the United States of America

Cover design by Christian Fuenfhausen

Author photo by Leanne Allison,

Interior design by Jennifer Shontz

13 14 15 16 17   5 4 3

Milkweed Editions, a nonprofit publisher, gratefully acknowledges sustaining support from Anonymous; Emilie and Henry Buchwald; the Bush Foundation; the Patrick and Aimee Butler Family Foundation; CarVal Investors; the Dougherty Family Foundation; the Ecolab Foundation; the General Mills Foundation; the Claire Giannini Fund; John and Joanne Gordon; William and Jeanne Grandy; the Jerome Foundation; Dorothy Kaplan Light and Ernest Light; Constance B. Kunin; Marshall BankFirst Corp.; Sanders and Tasha Marvin; the May Department Stores Company Foundation; the McKnight Foundation; a grant from the Minnesota State Arts Board, through an appropriation by the Minnesota State Legislature, a grant from the National Endowment for the Arts, and private funders; an award from the National Endowment for the Arts, which believes that a great nation deserves great art; the Navarre Corporation; Debbie Reynolds; the Starbucks Foundation; the St. Paul Travelers Foundation; Ellen and Sheldon Sturgis; the Target Foundation; the Gertrude Sexton Thompson Charitable Trust (George R. A. Johnson, Trustee); the James R. Thorpe Foundation; the Toro Foundation; Moira and John Turner; United Parcel Service; Joanne and Phil Von Blon; Kathleen and Bill Wanner; Serene and Christopher Warren; the W. M. Foundation; and the Xcel Energy Foundation.

The Library of Congress provided the following catalog information for the hardcover edition:

Heuer, Karsten.

Being caribou : five months on foot with an Arctic herd / Karsten Heuer.

p. cm.

Includes bibliographical references

ISBN 1-59785-010-0

1. Grant's caribou—Arctic regions—Anecdotes. 2. Human-animal relationships. 3. Heuer, Karsten. I. Title

QL737.U55H48 2005

599.65'8—dc22

2005024484

CIP

This book is printed on acid-free paper.

contents

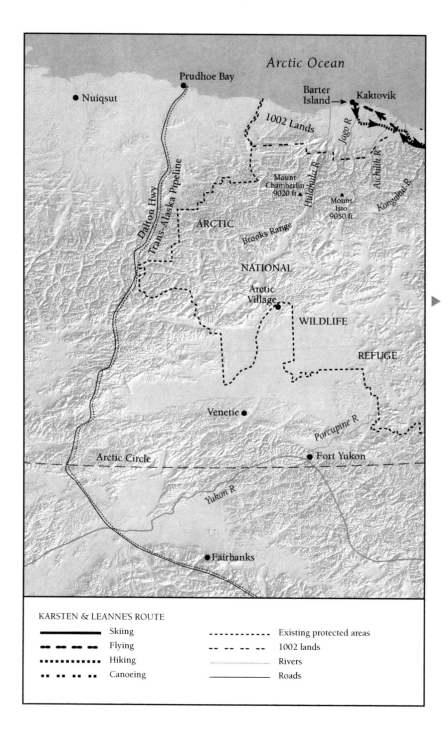

Arctic Ocean

Prudhoe Bay

Nuiqsut

Barter
Island → Kaktovik

1002 Lands

Jago R

Dalton Hwy

Trans-Alaska Pipeline

Mount
Chamberlin
9020 ft

Hulahula R

Mount
Isto
9050 ft

Aichilik R

Kongakut R

ARCTIC

Brooks Range

NATIONAL

Arctic
Village

WILDLIFE

REFUGE

Venetie

Porcupine R

Arctic Circle

Fort Yukon

Yukon R

Fairbanks

KARSTEN & LEANNE'S ROUTE

▬▬▬▬▬ Skiing	┄┄┄┄┄┄	Existing protected areas
▬▬ ▬▬ ▬▬ Flying	▬ ▬ ▬ ▬	1002 lands
▪▪▪▪▪▪▪▪▪▪ Hiking	┄┄┄┄┄┄	Rivers
▪▪ ▪▪ ▪▪ ▪▪ Canoeing	▬▬▬▬▬	Roads

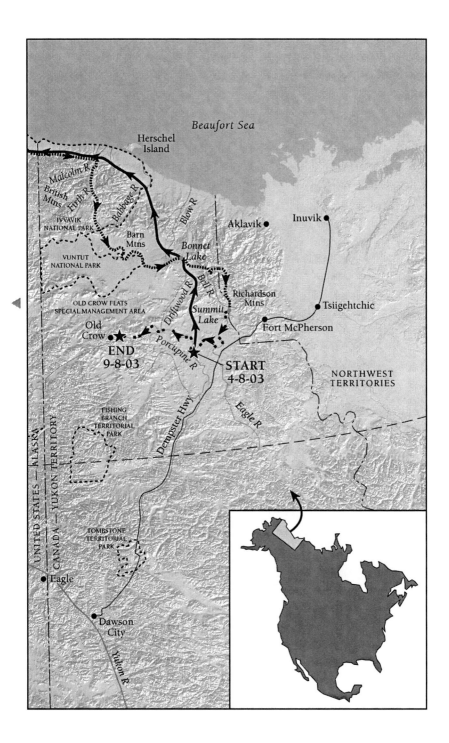

for the caribou and zev

With fresh trails striping the slope behind them, Leanne and Karsten climb yet another pass in an effort to stay with the postcalving herd in the foothills of the British Mountains, Yukon Territory, June 2003.

We need another and a wiser and perhaps a more mystical concept of wild animals. Remote from universal nature, and living by complicated artifice, man in civilization surveys the creatures through the glass of his knowledge and sees thereby a feather magnified and the whole image in distortion. We patronize them for their incompleteness, for their tragic fate for having taken a form so far below ourselves. And therein we err, greatly err. For the animal shall not be measured by man. In a world older and more complete than ours they move finished and complete, gifted with extensions of the senses we have lost or never attained, living by voices we shall never hear. They are not brethren, they are not underlings; they are other nations, caught with ourselves in the net of life and time, fellow prisoners of the splendour and the travail of the earth.

—Henry Beston, *The Outermost House*

prologue

We were surrounded. Waves of thick fog blew over the 20-mile-wide plain separating us from the Arctic Ocean, and in the intermittent clearings I glimpsed more and more grizzly bears. A big male slept on the riverbank, two adults nosed into the mist toward me, and 200 yards away, a mother with newborn cubs angled for the beach where we'd landed the rafts. I jabbed at the rusty siding of the dilapidated Water Survey cabin where we'd taken refuge, then yanked at the steel mesh bolted over the two small windows. Solid. And judging from the muddy paw prints smeared across every outside wall, the small 12-by-15-foot tin building in the middle of the open tundra had survived probing, rubbing bruins before. But I gave the hinges and handle of the door a good tug just in case as I stepped inside.

"Five more bears," I said, shaking the rime from the hood of my parka.

Steve looked up from the cloud of steam where he cooked a pot of noodles over the small camp stove and cupped a hand over his ear.

"Five more bears," I repeated, trying not to sound too surprised. I didn't know what was normal here. It was my first patrol down the Firth River and my first year as a seasonal warden in northern Canada's remote Ivvavik National Park. Steve Travis, on the other hand, was a seven-year veteran in the area and had made the 90-mile-long rafting trip down the Firth's twisting canyons more than thirty times. I searched his face for a reaction, but he only pulled on his wool hat and slipped out the door. It was 11:00 PM and dinner would have to wait.

The fog was beginning to lift, and by the time we scrambled onto the roof to look around, the view held seven bears, along with half a dozen golden eagles wheeling in and out of the rising clouds. I trained my binoculars on the farthest grizzly, a dark-coated animal with a hitching limp, and as I did, something on the slope behind it moved. I fiddled with the focusing ring while a tuft of grass slid sideways. A bush drifted downhill. Suddenly the whole slope was alive.

"Caribou!" I gasped.

Steve was already counting. "A few hundred," he guessed, but the dissipating clouds revealed more animals with each passing second. "Times fifty," he corrected half a minute later, but even that wasn't enough to account for what was unfolding before our eyes. It was late June 2001—just after the summer solstice—and as the midnight sun loosened the patchwork of mist around us, we found ourselves amid a sea of animals coursing northwest. Caribou cows and their newborn calves dotted every hillside and skyline, pouring over dark rocky slopes and lingering snowdrifts in waves and streams that spread like shadows toward the Firth River. By the time the wind shouldered us off the roof and back into the cabin, we had counted close to ten thousand, as well as twenty-four golden eagles, two foxes, thirteen ravens, a pair of rough-legged hawks, one peregrine falcon, countless gulls and terns, and eight grizzly bears. Even Steve was awestruck.

Although we'd had a long and difficult day on the river, it was impossible to sleep for much of that night. There was too much light, too much energy—too many life-and-death struggles unfolding around us—to justify rest. Group after group of grunting cows spurred hesitant newborns over the canyon rim. Cries of protest drifted up from the river as the young struggled in the first big swim of their life, the air filling with bellows and bleats as the current tore orderly strings of animals into a spreading chaos of calfless mothers and motherless calves. Mismatched animals pulled themselves onto the rocks and raced up and down the opposite shoreline. Lone calves disappeared over the horizon; distressed mothers plunged back into the water; and the eagles and grizzlies patrolled the gravel bars, waiting for those calves that were still struggling in the whirlpools to wash up.

Wanting to share the experience, I called my fiancée, Leanne Allison, on the satellite phone and tried to describe the scene: eight grizzly bears, thousands of caribou, a family of foxes yipping on the far side of the river, and Steve and I in the middle of it—the only people for hundreds of miles. When another group of animals thundered past, I held the phone out toward them, but the distance was too great. She was in the city of Vancouver, British Columbia; I was in the wilds of the northern Yukon, and the words and muffled sounds weren't enough to communicate the power of the migration. And yet there was something in my voice, she later told me, that said the lives we'd recently committed to living together were about to change.

The seed of the idea to follow the caribou was planted the next morning when the last animals crossed the river, climbed the ridge above us, and disappeared. After being immersed in caribou for the previous forty-eight hours, the silence that came behind them was almost unbearable. There were no grunts or snorts drifting up from the canyon, no screeches or calls from the peregrine falcons and eagles that, just hours earlier, had wheeled above. If not for the few despondent cows still searching for their lost calves, I might have thought it had all been a dream. But it couldn't have been, for no matter how fleeting the migration was, its energy had passed right through me, and in its absence was a space, loneliness, and yearning where none had existed before.

I pushed my raft into the water and watched as the last few animals disappeared over the ridge. Where were they going, I wondered, where had they come from, and what other dramas were already unfolding in the next valley?

But the river pulled me north toward the coast, not west along the foothills. For the time being, my curiosity would have to wait.

I was overcome with a strange sense of separation as the bush plane lifted us off the ocean spit a day later, and the feeling of leaving something important behind intensified when we touched down in the Northwest Territories town of Inuvik and I reentered what seemed another world. Trucks zipped back and forth on the dusty main street, while on the outskirts of the Native town of 3,000 people, men coiled rolls of seismic cable in fenced compounds filled with heavy machinery used in the quickening search for Arctic oil. Teenagers—Inuvialuit, white, Gwich'in—chatted on cell phones outside the local convenience store, and the sounds of Frosty's nightclub reverberated into the late hours while the sun circled overhead. I wandered through all of it in a daze, shuffling to and from the office where I sat at a keyboard and reduced everything—including the caribou migration—to numbers and map locations in a series of neatly typed reports. It was as though I'd crossed a line somewhere, a line that separated the busy node of human enterprise from the rhythms of the natural world, and the best I could do to lessen that boundary was read as much as possible about the animals that had so entranced me just days before.

The 123,000-member Porcupine Caribou Herd, it turns out, is the most well-studied caribou herd in the world, and I found no shortage of reports, books, and maps to pore over in the evenings. I learned about birth and death rates, preferred foods, and the relative importance of caribou in the modern-day diets of the Gwich'in, Inuvialuit, and Inupiat people in the thirteen communities scattered throughout its range. I read summaries of the movements of radio-collared animals, of archaeological reports that put those movements in historical context, and for relief from all the numbers, I often finished the evenings with a Native story or poem. Waiting for sleep that was slow to come, I lay in bed trying to cobble together all the numbers, histories, and myths. How the average caribou cow covers 2,800 miles a year; how 27,000-year-old trails continue to be used by caribou today; and how a Gwich'in man once made a pact to forever coexist with the caribou by exchanging a piece of his beating heart for one from a live bull.

But it was what I read about the Porcupine Caribou Herd's future that really kept me awake. Unlike other caribou herds in the western Arctic, their numbers are dwindling—down from 178,000 animals in the 1980s to 123,000 in 2001—and, to make matters worse, a long-standing proposal for oil and gas development in the heart of their Alaskan calving grounds was gathering momentum. Nobody could account for the current decline in the herd's numbers—global warming, increased hunting, airborne pollutants, predators, or simple natural fluctuation were all hypotheses that had been forwarded—but there was unanimous agreement among scientists that development in their calving grounds would negate recovery or, worse, accelerate their decline. It's like throwing a dart at the herd's most sensitive habitats and hitting the bull's eye, one biologist had told me. Of all the areas in their 96,000-square-mile range, this is one that should be left alone.

To the casual observer of maps, there isn't an issue. There can't be: the area immediately west of the Yukon's Ivvavik National Park is Alaska's Arctic National Wildlife Refuge, a name that infers protection for the American portion of the herd's calving grounds. Further investigation, however, reveals a different story. In order for the bill that established the refuge to pass in 1980, U.S. President Jimmy Carter was forced to make a last-minute compromise. Section 1002 of the act outlined that additional research was needed before Congress would designate a key 1.5-million-acre parcel along the coastal plain as part of the larger wilderness area. The reason was obvious: not only did the 1002 parcel of land contain the caribou's core calving grounds, but underneath it geologists suspected one of the largest reserves of oil in the entire United States. A decades-old battle was born.

I leafed through a summary of what had happened in the intervening years, hoping a resolution had been found, but the issue had only grown more complex. Further study had found the contested area to be not only critical to the caribou but important for a number of other animals as well. It is breeding and nesting habitat for 130 species of migratory birds from seven continents; it contains the best and highest concentration of onshore denning sites for the entire Beaufort Sea population of polar bears; and it is key birthing and rearing habitat for musk oxen, foxes, lemmings, and a host of small mammals that live in the area year-round. And then there is the issue of Native culture. The Gwich'in people, for whom caribou continue to be a mainstay of dietary and spiritual life, had filed a complaint to the United Nations that the proposed development would violate the International Charter of Human Rights. Meanwhile, in their offices and laboratories, corporate economists and geologists refined their forecasts for financial profit no matter the ecological and cultural costs.

Behind all this, of course, were the politics. Since being established, the Arctic National Wildlife Refuge had been subject to a partisan tug-of-war. Prowilderness Democrats sided with the Gwich'in, while prodevelopment Republicans, such as Ronald Reagan and the father-and-son Bush dynasty, pushed hard on behalf of the oil companies. From the caribou's perspective, the latest alignment of power in the United States—ex-oilman George W. Bush taking charge of the Oval Office in 2001 and the Republican Party controlling both the U.S.

Congress and Senate—was the most dangerous in years. Indeed, within the first few months of George Jr. taking office, four separate bills and amendments were introduced on Capitol Hill to open the refuge to development, each supported by then governor of Alaska, Frank Murkowski. And with the smell of royalty revenues thick in the air, his support was more than talk. Using $15 million of state funds, he helped finance an aggressive advertising and lobbying campaign for such oil giants as Chevron, Exxon, British Petroleum, and Conoco Phillips to further their cause.

Fortunately, a powerful opposition had mounted against the corporate interests. Environmental heavyweights such as the Sierra Club, the Wilderness Society, and World Wildlife Fund had joined smaller groups including the Alaska Wilderness League, the Yukon's Caribou Commons, and the Gwich'in Nation in a fight that had quickly grown into one of the largest environmental issues in North America. Campaigns had been planned and executed and celebrities such as Robert Redford had come forward in a collective effort that had successfully launched the issue into the American mainstream. As a result, every bill, amendment, and rider aimed at opening the Arctic National Wildlife Refuge for oil development had been defeated, although some by only very narrow margins.

Unfortunately, the battle was far from over. With the September 11, 2001, attacks on New York's World Trade Center fueling his cause, President Bush was using the new currency of fear to prop up what had been a questionable proposal from the start.

"We need to develop ANWR to reduce our dependence on rogue Middle Eastern states," he'd said in a 2002 speech to Congress, according to *Time* magazine, not mentioning how, by his own government's optimistic estimates, such extreme measures would serve to reduce that dependence on foreign oil from 69 percent to only 65 percent once ANWR reserves came on-stream. Nor had he said anything about the U.S. Geological Survey's calculations, which estimated the oil under the refuge would amount to no more than a six-month to one-year supply of total U.S. demand for oil. Keeping the speech on the familiar ground of homeland security, George W. argued for a plan that wouldn't really do anything except make a few more of his friends and business acquaintances even wealthier. Victims such as wildlife and Native people were minor obstacles at best.

It was a classic development-versus-conservation dilemma, and it had attracted plenty of media attention. Cover stories had run in *Time, National Geographic, Vanity Fair,* and a host of other magazines, and numerous documentaries had aired on television. But as I read and watched all of these, I realized I wasn't hearing the voice of the caribou. It was always the experts doing the talking, citing numbers and statistics that can't really be compared: Six months' worth of oil versus 27,000 years of migration. The culture of about 4,000 caribou-eating Gwich'in versus the financial benefits to a handful of company executives and shareholders. Millions of mammals and birds versus billions of barrels of oil. Nowhere was there a hint of what I'd felt out there on the tundra. Nowhere did I find the story of the caribou herd itself.

It was a little later the following summer, July not June, when Steve and I ran into caribou crossing the Firth River again, this time about 30 miles upstream of the Water Survey cabin, in the canyons of the British Mountains. Swollen with rain, the already treacherous stretch of white water had become a froth of muddy runoff, and when the first few caribou approached the riverbank, the floodwaters stopped them cold. Pulling hard against the current, we oared our way to the opposite shore, tied up the boats, and scrambled up to the canyon rim.

There was only so much time the lead animals could hesitate before the pressure of those piling in from behind sent them plunging in. Where they entered seemed a matter of luck more than choice, some selecting a stretch of flat water, others beginning their swim just a few strokes shy of a roiling set of rapids, pulling through a surge of twisting slots and bucking ledges that would have made every white-water rafter's mouth go dry. But mixed in with the miraculous swims were some tragic struggles. Heads heavy with antlers, a few of the big bulls got their shovel-like tines caught in the current, which snapped their heads and bodies around in whirlpools, sending them spinning downstream like dry leaves. Their wide, paddling hooves were useless against such turbulence, and soon they were pinballing down the canyon walls, flushing out of sight.

Only a few hundred caribou crossed that time, and when the rain stopped and the river level dropped a few days later, Steve and I continued our patrol downstream to the Arctic coast. We expected to come across a few carcasses, but what we found were dozens, each claimed by a hungry bear. A lone adult grizzly fed knee-deep in the rushing water; a mother with two full-grown cubs tore at a carcass splayed across a sandbar; and a big male hoarded five drowned caribou under a cliff, its bloodied face peering at us from behind pickets of fleshy, shining ribs. After several tense waits and the ignition of a few noisemakers, we reached the coast safely three days later and, while waiting for the plane, compared notes: thirty-odd carcasses, nineteen bears, and more eagles, ravens, jaegers, and hawks than we could count.

That's the story of the caribou, I thought to myself as arctic terns, king eiders, and a host of other birds splashed down between icebergs. That's the surge of life and death that all the magazine articles and television documentaries had failed to capture. The worth of the contended calving grounds—the 1002 lands, as they're called—was not to be found in numbers of barrels of oil or Native people or even caribou that depended on that particular swath of land but, rather, in the sheer effort and risk for the animals to migrate there and back from their wintering grounds each year. Four mountain ranges, hundreds of passes, dozens of rivers, countless grizzly bears, wolves, mosquitoes, and Arctic storms—those were the measures, that was the story, and the time had come to put it all together and try to bring it alive.

The day after I returned to Inuvik, Leanne arrived home from her own trip among the caribou. After joining me in the Arctic earlier that spring, she'd landed a contract with a Gwich'in youth project to create a video documenting what the caribou meant to them. Blue eyes sparkled in her tanned face as she told me all that had happened during her two-week stint filming in the Arctic National Wildlife Refuge, describing dramas not unlike what Steve and I had experienced only a few ridges away. Too excited to hold back any longer, I blurted out what had been brewing in my mind.

"We should follow them."

Leanne's smile vanished as she stared at me. "What?"

"Follow them," I repeated.

"Where?"

"Everywhere."

She paused to digest what I'd said. We'd talked in previous months about trying to do something that would make a difference in the decades-old issue, but she wasn't expecting this. "You mean migrate with the herd?"

"Exactly."

"For how long?"

I shrugged my shoulders. "However long it takes. Four, five, seven months—however long it takes them to get from the winter range to calving grounds and back."

Leanne paused again, trying to absorb the scale and magnitude of my proposal. We'd done a big trip before. In 1999 she'd joined me for the latter (and tougher) half of a 2,200-mile-long hike from

Yellowstone to the Yukon, promoting and assessing a plan to link parks and reserves along the Rocky Mountains with wildlife corridors (the Y2Y Conservation Initiative). That trek had been monumental in its scope and difficulty, but a trip with the caribou would be even more challenging. The Y2Y journey had merely symbolized where wildlife might move; the caribou trip would actually follow them, putting us at the mercy of their every move.

"We wouldn't know our route ahead of time," proclaimed Leanne as she worked through the logistics in her head.

I nodded and agreed. There are some patterns in the way the caribou migrate, but they can't be predicted, much less mapped, from year to year. Being caribou means not having fixed goals, objectives, or destinations. Our task would be to follow them, move like them, act like them, perhaps even think like them, and see what we learned along the way.

"What about food caches? There isn't a road or trail in their range."

What she said was true. Other than the two-lane gravel road that cut through a corner of their winter range, there was no ground access into the 96,000-square-mile area they roamed each year. Plus we'd have to devise a method for keeping our food out of the clutches of all those bears.

"We'd need a satellite phone," I admitted. "We'd have to call in our position for a resupply whenever we ran out of food."

"You mean planes?" she asked.

"They're cheaper than helicopters."

Leanne considered some traveling and camping specifics. "We'll have to start out on skis and sleep on snow for the first month or so. We'll have to melt snow and ice for water." She paused for a few seconds and winced. "We'll have to carry tons of stove fuel."

"Sometimes we'll have a small campfire on gravel and sandbars," I suggested.

I watched as the scope of the trip began to capture Leanne's imagination. Having worked on glaciers in Antarctica, scaled Canada's highest peak with the first all-women's expedition, and climbed some of South America's highest volcanoes, she was no stranger to executing a grand adventure. Within minutes her tentativeness had given way to excitement.

"We'd have to raise funds."

"And cook, dry, and package wheelbarrows of food," I added as a surge of energy filled the living room where we sat.

She nodded, already honing in on the finer details. "We won't need a water filter, but we'll need a way to keep the phone charged."

"Solar panel," I shot back.

Her face lit up at the prospect of being able to charge batteries. "I could take a video camera and film while you photograph and write."

I remembered some of the reports I'd read the previous winter, especially those that describe average caribou movements of 15 to 20 miles a day.

"Maybe, but we might not be doing anything except trying to keep up."

Leanne nodded. Having been out on the tundra for the last two weeks, she knew the walking wasn't anything like the mountain trails we'd followed in the Rocky Mountains. A good day's progress in the soft, wet, and hummocky Arctic tundra was often just a few miles. But she had also experienced the energy of the caribou, and that feeling was enough for her, as it was for me, to offset any reservations. Leanne turned to me with a smile.

"When do we leave?"

A necessary first step in any project in the Arctic is to consult with the numerous groups that might be affected, and when it comes to the Porcupine Caribou Herd, there is no shortage of stakeholders with which to consult: the Yukon Fish and Wildlife Management Board, the North Slope Game Council, various departments in the governments of Yukon Territory and the Northwest Territories, the Alaska Department of Fish and Wildlife, the Arctic National Wildlife Refuge, Parks Canada, the Inuvialuit hunter and trapper committees in Inuvik and Aklavik, and the Gwich'in renewable resource boards in those towns as well as the Northwest Territories communities of Tsiigehtchic and Fort McPherson and Old Crow, Yukon Territory. For the rest of that summer and fall, we met with as many of these groups as possible, and for those we didn't, we sent letters outlining our plan to migrate with the caribou the following spring.

"Unfortunately we don't have the legal authority to stop you," began a written answer from the Inuvialuit Game Council.

"I hope you learn all you're hoping to find out in a couple of days, because that's how long it'll take for the caribou to leave you behind!" laughed a Gwich'in man after I'd presented our proposal at a meeting in Tsiigehtchic.

Leanne and I couldn't help but feel the cynicism. And who could blame them? What we proposed was among the crazier schemes put forth in a long line of white explorers who had come north before us, many of whom had died. But something kept us going—smiles from some of the people we talked to and words uttered quietly, after the official meetings were over, in the hallways and parking lots outside.

"You'll see things no one has seen before," whispered an elder after a Hunters and Trappers Committee meeting in Aklavik, Northwest Territories. He was a whale of a man, a foot taller and 200 pounds heavier than I, and when he gently squeezed my arm, a wave of shivers shot right through my shoulder and down my spine. "Things *no one* has seen," he repeated wistfully.

Everybody's opinion mattered, but for Leanne and me, it was the opinions of the residents in the small fly-in village of Old Crow that mattered most. Situated near some of the more common points where the migrating Porcupine Herd crosses their namesake river, it is a community where, unlike most others we'd visited, the ties between the land and people haven't yet unraveled. On every kitchen table was a bowl of dried caribou meat, on most porches was a caribou skin drying, and in every household sat a rifle, ready in anticipation of the news that animals were coming out of the nearby hills. But it was more than a meat-on-the-table relationship, for as I stepped off the plane and walked the six dirt streets, the conversations I overheard referred to the animals with a reverence I had not witnessed any-where else. As though the caribou were friends, not animals, friends that could always be counted on to arrive when the people needed them most.

It was July 2002, and I was there to pitch our project to the North Yukon Renewable Resources Council, a committee of six residents who advised their government (the Vuntut Gwich'in First Nation) on fish, wildlife, and forestry issues within their traditional territory. Sitting apart from the table where the six councilors met, I waited as they sifted through financial statements, reviewed the results from a count of the latest salmon run, and discussed a report about the dwindling firewood supply around town. Finally, after an hour, and with two of the six councilors fast asleep, it was my turn to present.

Their eyes didn't stay closed for long. In the time it took me to introduce the idea and trace a rough 1,000-mile-long arc to the Arctic Coast and back on the map that hung on the wall, everyone was wide awake and leaning forward in their chairs. These were trappers, dog mushers, hunters, and travelers I was talking to, not bureaucrats, and they knew that the roadless, trail-less, structureless expanse I referred to was no walk in the park. Swamps, muskeg, mud bogs, bears, bugs, raging rivers, stabbing cold, and thin ice. They had all experienced at least some of it, and yet it was excitement that filled the room, not skepticism. When I finished, an electricity was in the air.

The vice chairman, a burly man with a black face and gnarled hands from more than fifty years outdoors, got up and spoke:

"Well," he said after sipping his coffee, "this man came here today with a brave idea, wondering if we can support him. Are there any questions?"

"What sort of experience do you have?" asked the chairman.

I listed my credentials as a park warden and a wildlife biologist, told of some of the skiing, climbing, and hiking expeditions Leanne and I had been on, then finished with a mention of the eighteen-month-long Yellowstone to Yukon hike.

He raised his eyebrows. "Yeah, but what Arctic experience?"

"Not much," I admitted. "Between the two of us, Leanne and I have spent only about two months on the tundra." I didn't mention that the majority of that experience was gained while sitting on the pontoon of a well-stocked raft.

The vice chairman cleared his throat as the quieter of the two women on the council giggled and the two sleepers laughed.

Pointing around the room, he said, "Each one of us has been to Washington, D.C., and elsewhere in the States to lobby for protection of the calving grounds. We've written letters. We've done conference calls." He waved a hand at the computer on a nearby desk. "We've even emailed."

Everyone laughed as he took a deep breath.

"This trip you're talking about ... it's a good idea. It's time somebody from the outside came and told the story of these caribou and our people. The real story."

He sidled up to me and slapped my shoulder.

"A lot of us are frustrated with this issue. If you pull this trip off, it might just be what saves this herd."

The smile I was wearing when I walked out of that meeting only broadened as I spent more than an hour on the porch of the tribal office that afternoon, killing time until the plane came to take me back to Inuvik the next day. It was the unofficial meeting place in town, a south-facing porch with two comfortable benches where everyone stopped for a smoke or coffee on their way to and from the post office or to use the public computers just inside the door. As the afternoon passed, I sat and talked with First Nation Councilors, carpenters, elders, and everyone in between, repeating my story for anyone willing to listen. There was genuine excitement from most people, and save for one person everyone laughed or at least smiled. Only the old man who hadn't moved on the bench across from me stayed silent, listening carefully to all that was said with a stony look on his face. Finally, when everyone else had left and we were alone, he opened his mouth and uttered the words I wouldn't forget.

They were couched in warnings about times he'd seen caribou moving hundreds of miles without stopping, crossing the frozen lakes of Old Crow Flats with their eyes closed, sleeping as they walked. And in stories about earlier people who had followed them on snowshoes and foot—his grandfather and his ancestors before him—not because they'd wanted to, but because it was what they did to survive.

"Back then things were different," he said, waving an arm as another group of kids clambered through the doors to use the Internet. "Not as crazy as now but more intense."

I nodded, encouraging him to continue, not quite ready for what he said next.

"Back then people could talk to caribou, and caribou could talk to people."

From the way he looked at me after he said it, I knew he'd divulged something not often shared. I thanked him, trying to shroud my disbelief. I didn't understand what he'd just said, and as far as I was concerned, I never would. He was the descendant of Athapaskan hunters who had roamed the Arctic forests and tundra for thousands of years; I, the son of German immigrants who had raised a family in the city of Calgary, Alberta. The cultural gap between us was too big to ever close.

Or so I thought.

Fourteen months later, after skiing and walking more than 1,000 miles with and without caribou, I would return to Old Crow knowing exactly what he meant.

APPROXIMATE WINTER RANGE OF PORCUPINE CARIBOU HERD

setting off

To all that has run its course, and to the vast unsayable
numbers of beings abounding in Nature,
add yourself gladly, and cancel the cost.
　　　—Rainer Maria Rilke, *Sonnets to Orpheus,* Part Two, XIII

We stood on the frozen Porcupine River, struggling to say goodbye. A well-trod caribou trail left the ice not far from where we'd cached freshly butchered meat the night before, and after Leanne and I helped Randall and James load their toboggans, the four of us stood where the snowmobile and animal trails diverged.

"Well, this is it," I said.

"This is it," Randall repeated. We all waited a few awkward moments for something wise or profound to follow, but everything had been covered the night before.

"See you in the fall then?" I asked.

Randall chuckled. "Yeah, Creator willing, we'll see you in the fall."

In the fall. The words rang in my ears as the sound of the snowmobiles faded and Leanne and I clipped on skis, hoisted bulging packs, and strode off. Half a year and two seasons away. We'd written it down over and over in funding proposals, permit applications, customs declarations, and instructions to bush pilots before leaving, but now that we'd been flown, towed by snowmobile, and dropped off in the middle of a vast, foreign landscape, the scale of our endeavor hit with an unwelcome weight. I looked at the forest of tiny trees blanketing the surrounding hillsides, felt the huge, frozen river groan and crack beneath me, then pushed toward the snow-covered shore, dizzy and overwhelmed.

The view from the plane window flying from Inuvik to Old Crow a few days earlier hadn't helped. Despite the bright, sunny weather, what had unfolded beneath us appeared to be the most inhospitable place on earth. Not a tree in the buckle of mountains and tight valleys. Not a speck of color in the folds of white tundra. Nothing moving across an ocean of snowdrifts and wind scoops visible from 15,000 feet up in the air. An hour later, after we'd flown south of tree line and the plane touched down on the gravel strip in Old Crow, I'd hesitated, unsure whether I wanted to get off.

Once I had, there was no turning back. No sooner had Leanne and I stepped inside the one-room airport than locals who recognized me from my visit the summer before waved and approached.

"Don't leave now; the caribou won't be through for another month," one man warned.

"The caribou have already left. You're too late!" another exclaimed.

"If you go now, they'll take you in circles," began a respected elder. "Stay in town. Stay warm and comfortable. Leave when the bulls come through in May."

Looking out the window at the thermometer made his suggestion all the more tempting. Even though it was April 7—spring by southern standards—it read minus 35 degrees Fahrenheit.

A long and somewhat confusing chain of differing opinions had finally led us to Randall Tetlichi's door a day and a half later, and it was there that all the speculation and conjecture stopped about where we might find caribou. After listening to a shortened version of our well-rehearsed pitch for information, the squat, bowlegged man said he'd been hunting the day before, then invited us inside.

"I went to the calving grounds a few years back," he said after we'd lunched together on caribou soup. "Not quite what you're talking about—I got dropped by a plane—but I was there for the same reason."

"And?" I asked after a long silence.

"And what?" he quietly asked back.

"What did you find?"

A shadow ran across his weathered face, then it passed and he laughed.

"Well, I guess you'll see when you get there."

"*If* we get there," I corrected. The differing opinions, the weather, and the overview from the plane had all taken their toll. But Randall wouldn't have anything to do with my wavering words.

"If you think you won't, you won't. If you know you can, you will."

I looked at him stirring a pot of caribou bones on the stove and caught the tail end of a steady, piercing stare. He looked in the pot, then back at me, a thin smile creeping onto his whiskered face.

"So do you want to leave tomorrow?"

Leanne and I exchanged hopeful glances.

"I don't know," I said. "Should we?"

Randall shrugged. "I don't know either." We all laughed.

"You said you were hunting," Leanne began.

Randall nodded. "Yesterday."

"How many? What were they doing?" I wanted to ask more questions but held back.

"Hundreds," answered Randall. "And more coming. I don't know if it's the migration, but it might be. They were really traveling."

I pulled out the map that was already dog-eared and ripped from showing it to so many people while asking their advice, but this time there was none of the usual oblique gesturing and generalizations. Randall pointed to the spot without hesitation: along the Porcupine River 40 miles east of town, where the Richardson Mountains rise up from the forested hills and begin their 300-mile run to the Arctic coast.

Step, pole plant, step, pole plant, step, pole plant, fall.

"What do you think?" I shouted back to Leanne after two hours of slow climbing.

"Not bad," she lied. I turned to gauge the look on her face, but as I did the trail collapsed beneath me, sending me careening headfirst into the snow.

The trail of hoofprints was one of many we'd found leaving the river that morning and, like the others, proved too narrow to ski. After trying numerous methods, we'd settled on walking inside the foot-wide trench, stumbling over our own feet with each step. It was awkward—like balancing along a slippery log—but it was the only viable option in a land where any snow not packed by animals was too weak to support our weight. Rotted by a winter of extreme cold, the snow had a sugarlike consistency that was nothing like the firm, settled snow we were accustomed to farther south. Venturing beyond the narrow line packed by single-file caribou meant wallowing up to our hips, with or without skis.

I dug myself out, took another dozen steps, then stopped to wait for Leanne, who cursed somewhere behind.

"Maybe we should've brought snowshoes after all," I said as she stumbled up.

"Maybe, but what does it matter now?"

She was right. When the sound of the snowmobiles had disappeared that morning, so too had the last opportunity for adjustments or substitutions. For the next four to seven months, we would be forced to live with the decisions we'd made about taking a tiny tent, only one sleeping bag to share between the two of us, and very little cooking fuel in the hopes we could have frequent small fires.

Time would tell about the first two decisions, but we weren't far up the first slope before we knew firewood wasn't going to be a problem, at least not for the first while. The spruce trees that looked so small and well spaced from the river closed around us in a maze of prickly trunks and intertwined limbs.

"I think being caribou means being gymnasts," muttered Leanne as she crawled through a tunnel of branches on all fours. I slithered after her, grunting as clumps of caribou hair fell off the trees that now snagged every buckle and strap on my pack. I staggered upright into the next opening, only to have the snow fail beneath my feet yet again. Casting aside my skis, I wriggled out of my pack's shoulder straps, climbed free of the newly created crater, then reached down 2½ feet and dug out the pack.

We were soaked, sweaty, and exhausted by the time we approached the top of the hill five hours later, and with an open bench beckoning just below the summit, we struck our first camp.

"We've hardly gone anywhere!" cried Leanne once we'd finished pitching the tent on the snow and taken a good look around. Below, the river snaked through the trees like a snowed-over highway, and down the middle of it was the snowmobile trail, still visible as a thick white line. I wanted to tell her it was an illusion, that the smaller trees, lower mountains, and clearer air created an alternate sense of scale. But the truth was, we hadn't done well.

April 10—Mason Hill, Richardson Mountains, Yukon—
Day One, and my body tells me we've gone farther over the last eight hours than the 3 miles that show

on the map. If I knew the whereabouts of the caribou, I'd have another measure, but judging from the tracks around us, it would only be worse. The hoofprints aren't as crisp as those we followed off the river this morning. We're farther behind now than we were at the beginning of the day.

I closed the journal and pulled on my down coat as tiny snores sounded beside me in the sleeping bag. From the small opening where Leanne had buried her head, puffs of steam rose and then crystallized in the cold air around me. I too was exhausted, but a combination of late-night Arctic sunshine and German worrying kept me sitting up and looking out the door. Using binoculars, I scoured the land for hidden animals and, when I found none, followed the river through every twist and turn that still bore the marks of the day before: the corner where James had stopped the snowmobile and launched into his speech, the straightaway where we'd first seen caribou, and the spot where he'd asked me to hand him his gun.

James Itsi couldn't be any more different from Randall: tall and thin, the sixty-something woodcutter wears his gray hair close-cropped instead of in a long ponytail and, unlike his soft-spoken friend, loves to talk. While Randall had silently readied his toboggan in Old Crow, James had chatted to me, to Leanne, to anyone else who happened past as we'd packed—leaving him scrambling when Randall started his snowmobile and, with a motion for Leanne to get on behind him, took off.

A half hour later, we finally left. James wanted me to ride on the back of the toboggan, not on his machine. I'd obliged but knew as we fishtailed out of town and down the riverbank that the arrangement wasn't going to last long. It was like riding a whip, and as James cornered onto the river ice, the sled of split boards, ripped canvas, and frayed rope skidded wide, hit a drift, bucked, then flipped.

"James!" I shouted as I picked myself up out of the snow. "James!"

The whine of the snowmobile grew fainter as he kept going, dragging all our carefully packaged food, fragile solar equipment, and lightweight skis sideways through the snow. Images of him catching up to Leanne and Randall with only a frayed rope behind him flashed through my head, along with a bird's-eye view of all our belongings scattered along the river for miles.

"James!" I screamed louder. "I'm off!"

Still he kept going, oblivious to what had happened, and he probably would have continued on had the toppled sled not caught another drift and dug in.

"What happened?" he asked, coming back to collect me after being jerked to a stop. He waved off my concerns, telling me to get back on the toboggan handles, and didn't looked back again.

Initially James seemed intent on catching Randall and Leanne, but after 20 miles of winding back and forth between the brushy riverbanks, he seemed happier to stop and point out the local landmarks. The hills that surround Old Crow were higher around us here, and he gestured to the clefts and benches where old fishing camps had once sat under rolling spruce and birch forests, with the beginnings of the Richardson Mountains looming behind.

"Mason Hill," he said, pointing to a treeless plateau. Squinting into the sun, I tried to decipher patterns I thought I saw on the snowy ridge. Before I could pose the question, however, James was beside me. "Caribou tracks," he said. "Fresh."

We were close, I could feel it, and as James walked back to the idling snowmobile, I found new strength to grip the bucking toboggan handles. But rather than hitting the throttle, he cut the engine. Swallowing my frustration, I waited as he wandered to where I stood—unprepared for what was to come.

This time James really wanted to talk. Not about landmarks, caribou tracks, or fishing camps, but about the predicament he and his family and nearly every other Gwich'in person was living with: the pull of modern-world economics and how it was changing the very values of traditional life. He had obviously heard enough from Randall to know what Leanne and I were up to, and as a northern aboriginal talking to a white southerner, he wanted to seize his chance to set us straight: Old Crow was more than a quaint village of caribou hunters, he told me, and the issue of whether or not to develop for oil and gas wasn't as clear-cut as we thought.

What got him started was the creek in front of us. It was where an old shortcut trail used to leave the river and cut east across the hills, linking Old Crow with the Gwich'in community of Fort McPherson 200 miles away. Judging by its overgrown condition, it hadn't been used in years.

"Instead of packing a trail on snowshoes, everybody goes around on the river on their fast skidoos," began James. "It's 40 miles extra, but nobody cares. They'll spend money they don't have on gas before they'll work. Nobody sweats anymore. Nobody even gets their own firewood—they hire me, an old man, instead."

"We were supposed to be better off with education—sending people away—but look where that got us: Sexual abuse. Loss of language. And still there aren't jobs. When young people graduate and come back, they take jobs I could have. So what does an old man do? I end up cutting and hauling firewood. I'm sixty-two years old!"

He stopped for a breather, looked at me, then launched into the heart of his argument.

"Maybe we should open up the calving grounds. We need jobs, money. Things have changed." He pointed again to the old, untouched trail. "Nobody hunts unless the path is already broken! The caribou will be fine," he assured me. "They're along the Dempster Highway all the time. They like that road. They like skidoo trails. A few pipelines won't matter."

James stopped. I thought of biological studies to refute what he'd said, but it wasn't the time or place to bring them up. What he was struggling with was a moral issue, one that few of us outsiders had ever thought about, and because of that, there was little I could say.

"Why shouldn't we have everything that everyone else does?" he asked. "Nice things from the store. You know what I'm talking about ... Freight is expensive. People are poor. They don't have enough to eat. Things aren't good." He paced to the end of the snowmobile and back to the handlebars, fingering at the pull cord while stamping a foot in the snow. "I've worked in oil camps," he said, hesitating. "On the drill rigs. They're warm, comfortable, have good food. Life is easy. That's why I'm so fit now; why, at sixty-two, I'm still a strong man."

James stopped to look at me again, but I remained quiet. Who was I to say that he and his daughters and his grandson shouldn't have everything everyone else did at the expense of nature? Who was I to talk about what was right and wrong, what was comfortable or not, with my new Gore-Tex pants and jacket and my camera and lenses slung around my hip? I looked at James, then up at the caribou trails. He followed my eyes, then walked back to the snowmobile.

"Well, we better get going," he said, grasping the pull cord.

I nodded and held on.

Three corners later, we ran headlong into a hundred caribou jogging toward us, agitated by something behind them we could scarcely make out: in the middle of the frozen river, Randall was alone on his snowmobile, towing a carcass to where Leanne stood waiting, with others splayed out near the shore.

"Quick, my gun!" James shouted as he hit the brake and wheeled off his machine. While he fumbled through his pockets for bullets, I untied the load and handed him the old, duct-taped rifle. Then I covered my ears.

There is nothing sporting about modern-day caribou hunting. While the first animal dropped, the rest continued toward us, jogging into James's bullets. Two, three, four shots echoed off the hillside and still they came, leaving two more adults in the snow and a bloody yearling quivering on frozen legs. It wasn't until a gut-shot adult pawed at the air and bucked a few times that a ripple of panic went through the herd. A fifth animal stumbled and crashed to the ice, a sixth, then James reloaded, but it was too late. The remaining animals escaped his range, and they climbed a hill on the opposite shore. Two injured caribou lay on the ice watching them but couldn't follow, and by the time James towed the five others to where I stood waiting, they too were dead. Seven still-steaming bodies lay before me, blood mixing with snow, a puddle of pink liquid growing at my feet.

Looking up at James, I managed a weak smile.

"Don't just stand there. Help!" he said, already cutting. Sick from the smell of gunpowder and fresh flesh, I fought back nausea, grabbed my knife, walked up to the nearest carcass, grabbed a handful of warm fur, and sliced in.

Butchering the animals helped. I wasn't good at it—my blade floundered between muscles and hide, its tip cutting unnecessarily as it searched for the cartilage between joints—but that didn't seem to matter much to James. Together, we were engaged in something elemental, something primitive, and it displaced everything that had weighed against our hearts and souls only an hour before. My nausea dissipated, and my hands and blade moved through the animal seemingly of their own accord as I drifted into a kind of trance.

"Hey, Carson."

I looked up.

"Yeah?"

"All those things we were talking about back there …?"

"Yeah?"

The tension that had clouded James's face before the hunt had lifted. He was beaming.

"This is what matters now," he said, hefting a chunk of meat in his hand. "This is what it means to be Indian."

As Leanne and I set off again the next morning, the images and textures of the butchering session were still fresh in my mind. It was hard not to think of all the advantages the caribou had over us: four legs instead of two; a lightweight, ultra-insulating coat of hollow hair instead of layers of constricting clothing; no frozen leather boots to pry onto their feet in the morning; and, most important of all, no pack. Hunching my shoulders, I braced myself as a foot slipped off the trail and the 70-pound load pitched me forward again.

What had impressed me the most while helping James butcher was the size of the animals' hearts, lungs, and leg muscles: four times as large as my own, yet packaged in a fine-limbed body that, when upright, didn't even reach my shoulders. Remembering the grace with which they'd moved even while hunted, I followed the tracks of the wide, splayed hooves before me, trying to mimic the light-footed gait with which the trail had been made. But I couldn't. Laden with satellite phone, cameras, solar panel, extra battery, food, clothes, and worries, I was too burdened to be anything close to caribou just yet.

If we'd seen animals that second morning, we might have been encouraged, but what we got were new problems that only compounded our doubts. Within an hour of leaving where we'd camped, the deep trench we'd been following since the day before split and went on to branch so many times that soon there was no real trail to follow at all. The whole forest floor was suddenly covered in prints and dugouts where the single-file animals had fanned out on their own to dig and feed.

"Now what?" asked Leanne.

I looked at the minefield of tracks, scat, and craters before us as a ball of uneaten lichen rolled past in the breeze. Stretching around both sides of the broad hillside, the trampled area was enormous—too big for a few thousand caribou to have snacked here before moving on. It was as if they'd stopped for days, not minutes; as if food and rest were what they'd been most interested in, not traveling. I felt an old panic rise in my chest. Were they milling more than migrating? Was it as someone in Old Crow had suggested? Had we left too soon?

The question of when to start following the caribou was one we'd agonized over all winter, and with good reason. More than any other decision, it would determine the success or failure of our trip. If the caribou indeed were migrating and we didn't go now, there was little chance of ever catching up. And if they weren't migrating and we did go now, we risked expending precious energy circling after them before they really started the long trip to the Arctic coast.

The problem was that migrating caribou and milling caribou are difficult to distinguish, especially from a distance. All winter, we had watched on the biologists' website as the herd's seven radio-collared animals moved from point to point in their winter range, drifting from west-central Yukon to the interior of Alaska and back again. It had been an atypical season. Instead of the herd settling into an area and staying put, factions had roamed from one feeding site to another, stopping only briefly before moving on. The resulting pattern was the source of our quandary: Was a northward movement the beginning of the long migration or just another in a long series of short, circling jaunts?

Historical reports hadn't helped much. The patterns of the last three decades showed that the spring migration had started anywhere between the beginning of February and May. I looked at records of snow depth, temperature, and winds for some correlation, but like the dozens of scientists who'd done the same before me, I couldn't find a pattern. When it comes to the start of the migration, the caribou are completely unpredictable.

Our start was based on a phone call from a friend in Old Crow. People were leaving town on snowmobiles, he'd said, and were returning the next day with meat in their sleds. He didn't know how many animals were involved, nor could he say how or even if they were moving. After looking one last time at the website and finding three of the seven radio-collared animals positioned just south of the Porcupine River, we headed for the Inuvik airport.

The uncertainty had continued right through our brief stopover in Old Crow and still lingered around the trapper's cabin where we holed up with Randall and James after the hunt.

"So what do you think?" I asked as more than a thousand animals wound down the river 200 yards from the porch where we all stood. "Are they migrating?"

Randall and James weren't looking to hunt—both of them had just gotten enough meat to feed their families until the fall—but they would never tire of watching. When a few more cows emerged from the trees and lay down, Randall cleared his throat.

"They look tired. As though they've traveled all day and all night."

James nodded but then shook his head a few seconds later when some of the animals trundled on. "I've seen them like this while they're circling," he countered. "It's hard to say."

In the end, it was a dream that convinced us it was time to follow the caribou—Leanne's dream—and the way it happened was almost too perfect to believe. After a night of listening to Randall's stories and advice for the journey ahead, I made Leanne a bed from an old caribou skin we'd found on the porch, then lay down on the floor beside her pondering everything Randall had said. There were stories of his growing up, of the many near misses he'd survived on countless hunts—elements of adventure that Leanne and I were already familiar with: examples of poor judgment, excessive hubris, lack of preparation, a collapse of mental strength.

But Randall also referred to things I couldn't relate to: ancestral spirits, dreams, visions—things his grandfather had accessed in his consistent predictions of where and when to find caribou next—like a deep instinct that resides in the land. A part of me shunned such notions, the part that had grown up in a city, trained as a scientist, and looked at the world through a rational and logical lens. But another part of me said that when it came time to follow caribou, we were going to need all the help we could get.

"Take good care of each other," Randall had summed up at the end of the evening. "Expect the unexpected. And always pay attention to your dreams."

I appreciated everything he told us and believed it all to be important, but I couldn't help but be skeptical when Leanne woke up the next morning babbling about her dream. It was all too convenient: months of uncertainty suddenly resolved because of what a stranger had told her the night before. But despite the look I flashed her, Leanne was adamant.

"It was spring," she recounted, struggling to contain her excitement. "The Porcupine River was breaking up. The ice was gone. A wide ribbon of green water rushed downstream."

Suspicious, I watched Randall for his reaction, but there was no judgment on his face, no hint of doubting, and none of my own disbelief.

"Well, I guess that's your answer," he'd said, smiling. "You better get going."

It took more than an hour of postholing and wading before we found a few threads of consolidated snow among the array of craters and circling paths, and we followed them out of the confusion of tracks to where they braided into a trail that led toward the ridge. But no sooner were we accustomed to balancing along a trench again than it began to soften underfoot. More splits, more forks, more lines spreading into another hundred-acre patch of soft snow, sending us floundering through the trees. After merging back onto the "freeway," we plowed into another field of muck. The exhausting cycle repeated itself, and the number of rest stops increased.

"You know how the Inuit apparently have hundreds of words to describe all the different kinds of snow?" Leanne remembered as we sat on our packs, catching our breath.

"Uh-huh," I answered, too tired to talk.

"Well, what about the Gwich'in?"

"What about them?"

"Do they have different words?"

"How should I know?"

Leanne absentmindedly stabbed the snow with a ski pole. Tiny avalanches ran down, covering our boots.

"Well, if they do, this stuff must be a swearword!"

I laughed and shouted out a list of possibilities in English as we lurched off once again.

By the end of the third day, we were exhausted. We went to bed sore, woke up stiff, and avoided talking about what we saw on the map. Five miles the second day, 7 miles on the third, and we were more tired than after days when we'd walked 30 miles on the mountain trails down south. But there was one thing that kept us going, a trend that, despite our slow progress, had already changed since the first day: the tracks we followed were getting fresher. All the feeding had slowed the caribou down.

It was a bittersweet situation, and it sent me fretting all over again. There was no way to define what a migrating caribou did or didn't look like, but my personal image didn't include animals that a couple of floundering humans could catch. I was happy we might finally see them but worried that when we did, they would abandon us in the sea of soft snow and, instead of migrating, veer south to feed.

Those fears were partially realized when we reached Salmon Cache Creek later that afternoon. The trail we followed was only one of dozens that funneled onto the frozen creek bed and turned 90 degrees, tracking east.

"Really fresh," I whispered to Leanne as we donned our skis and pushed with both poles up the alleyway of frozen urine and splintered ice. Thousands of animals had ascended the creek before us and, judging by the heavy scent hanging in the air, the last ones had passed not long before. But it was late—8:00 PM—and after turning a few corners without seeing anything, we decided that what hadn't happened in our first ninety-six hours of following caribou could wait another ten. Scarcely uttering a word between us, we found a flat piece of ice, pitched the tent on top of it, cooked a quick dinner, and promptly fell asleep.

Sounds woke me in the night. I listened for the wind brushing the trees, but it was something else that creaked, something walking on the ice. I nudged Leanne awake.

"Do you hear that?"

"Hear what?"

"That," I said as footsteps crunched closer. She wormed her upper body out of the sleeping bag, pulled off her balaclava, and listened. The sound was all around us. We lay there for a few minutes, eyes wide open, trying to figure how many animals lurked around the tent. Slowly I unzipped the door, one tooth at a time.

With a half-moon illuminating them, the figures looked more like ghosts than caribou—silver cutout shapes silhouetted against a green sky dancing with northern lights. Thirty animals were within view, more poured out of the trees every passing second, and we watched as each animal nosed the bank before entering onto a stage of glittering ice with a backdrop of emerald scarves. A few bedded down, but most milled around our camp, sniffing at our skis and poles, stopping to mouth the sweaty stains on our packs before pushing on. Chins propped on our makeshift pillows, Leanne and I grinned as the procession of furry legs and splayed hooves passed at eye level for twenty minutes. When the last animal disappeared, we pressed our ears to the tent floor and listened as the ice thumped with the tempo that would determine the rhythm of our own footsteps for the next five months.

I woke twice more that night to the sound of groups passing and once to a tremendous crash. It was 4:30 AM, light enough not only to see the groaning cow limp away but also for us to consider getting up and moving as well. The thought of squeezing into frozen boots and packing an icy tent sent me burrowing into the warm bag, however, and I dropped back to sleep nuzzled against Leanne. When I next opened my eyes, it was half past ten.

"Was that a dream?" Leanne asked as we extracted ourselves, heavy limb by heavy limb, from the tent. The sun had climbed high overhead, and the glare had transformed the shadowy, starlit scene into an ordinary frozen creek.

I pointed to the fresh tracks studding the ice all around us, saying with certainty it had been real.

"So what do you think now?" I asked, still consumed by the question. "Are we in the migration?"

Leanne gave a look that said she hadn't given it much thought. Slurping her tea, she pondered it for a few moments, then shoveled a spoonful of oatmeal into her mouth.

"I don't know," she answered after swallowing, "but maybe we'll find out today."

I was so consumed by the possibility of traveling with caribou that I thought nothing of shortcutting where their trails detoured off the frozen creek a mile later the next morning. Eager to make up time wherever possible, I overlooked the sudden change in ice color beneath me and blithely pushed toward the spot where I saw tracks reemerge from the trees.

"Don't follow!" I shouted a few strides later, when blue ice gave way to gray. Water poured around my ankles, and my knees were engulfed in slush, but it was already too late. Behind me, Leanne had also broken through the thin veneer of ice and was standing on the thicker layer beneath it, getting soaked by the water caught between.

"Overflow!" I barked, making for the shore as I searched to avoid the nearby spring. But no sooner had I lunged than I was pitched over, stopped by skis that wouldn't budge. Now up to my elbows as well as my knees, I crawled through the slurry of ice and slush on all fours, breaking through deeper before finally rolling onto the bank. Grabbing handfuls of snow, I padded my legs and arms, trying to get the snow to absorb the water from my clothes before it froze.

It had been cold earlier that morning—somewhere around minus 25 degrees Fahrenheit—and although the sun was out now, it lacked the strength to warm us for the cold hour that followed. Striking at dead branches on the surrounding trees with numb hands, I labored to gather a pile of tinder as Leanne struggled with the lighter. When a flame finally popped up from her white fingers, we nursed it into a roaring fire.

"Now we know why the caribou didn't go this way," said Leanne as she held her bare feet next to the flames. I wrung out my socks and poured the water from my boots as I sat across from her, watching columns of steam rise off our pants.

"Sorry."

She shrugged off any blame as she slammed her feet back into soaked boots. "Well, if we want to catch them, we can't afford to sit around all day."

We stayed warm and kept our things from freezing solid by moving faster than usual, and when the trail veered off the creek for the last time, a surge of renewed energy sent us climbing along the path to the next ridge. The caribou had turned north again, not south, and with each step we took, the likelihood that it was migrating and not milling caribou we were following spurred us on.

The view was incredible once we broke out of the trees, and we sat on top of the broad summit later that afternoon scanning in all directions as we nibbled broken crackers and frozen cheese. The snaking path of the Porcupine River was still visible in the hills behind, the rugged interior ranges of the Richardsons rose like white fins ahead, and to our left stretched a mottled ocean of forested islands and frozen lakes.

"Old Crow Flats?" Leanne asked, looking west over the flat expanse.

I nodded, then trained the binoculars north again, examining every cleft and angle in the buckled slopes for a hint of movement. The mountains were bigger, the valleys narrower, and the trees fewer than what we'd traversed so far, but in terms of animals, nothing had changed.

"You want the good news or the bad news first?" I asked a few minutes later.

Leanne brushed the crumbs off her hands and reached into the food bag for a fruit bar.

"The bad news," she mumbled, already chewing.

"Not an animal in sight."

She swallowed, took another bite, then traded me the rest for the binoculars.

"And the good?" she asked, raising them to her eyes.

"We can see where we're going for the next three days."

I watched her squint behind the lenses, her fingers adjusting the focusing ring to follow the trail dipping and rising through a maze of steepening ridges that every once in a while gave way to cliffs.

"Are you sure it wasn't goats that made that path?" she asked, looking back at me.

"No mountain goats in this part of the Yukon."

"No goats?"

"No goats."

Right," she said, squeezing a few fingers underneath her hat to scratch at the flattened curls beneath it. "I forgot."

The ridge was beautiful skiing for the first few miles—a catwalk of hard drifts that sent us sailing across the skyline and, except for the occasional boulder lurking below the surface, none of the usual rocks to clip and gouge our skis. But getting off it was problematic. Eroded by the creek that curved underneath it, the descending ridge started as a gentle slope but suddenly tumbled into a broken cliff. We took off our skis, tied them to our packs, and lowered ourselves from one ledge to the next, hand over hand.

"The reason there aren't goats around here is because of all the goatlike caribou," droned Leanne in a professorial voice. "A classic case of competitive exclusion."

Too nervous to laugh, I grunted through the moves she'd made look so easy, scratching for purchase with gloved fingers as another piece of rock crumbled in my grasp. Finally I was safely beside her, looking where she pointed at the tracks. Judging by the spaces between them, the caribou had negotiated the same vertical steps in leaps and bounds.

I'm not sure why we put our skis back on at that point—perhaps some of the courage and recklessness of the caribou had rubbed off on us—because we could have safely kicked steps down what became instead a hair-raising descent. Skittering on the edge of control, we cut across a wind-blasted slope that should have avalanched, then dropped into a couloir to sideslip what we should have rappeled. Somehow staying upright, I shot through an alleyway of protruding rocks guarding the bottom, but my speed was too great. One leg veered, the other shot forward, and when a ski tip caught, I knew it was all over but the crash.

"If it weren't for that face-plant at the bottom, I would have given you a perfect ten," Leanne laughed as she skimmed past me. I picked myself up and hurried out of the avalanche runout zone. Brushing off the last of the snow, I looked back at the three lines scrawled down the shadowy mountain face—Leanne's, the caribou's, and mine—and marveled at how we'd all survived.

> *April 15—Unnamed valley north of Salmon Cache Creek, Yukon*—Ice walkers, snow diggers, forest dwellers, and mountaineers. Day Six, and already the caribou have gone places I never thought possible. No slope is too steep, no forest too thick, no valley too long or deep. We are only one week into this months-long trip, and although we have yet to find a group of caribou to travel with, I'm already worn down. Muscles ache and cramp as I lie in this sleeping bag, and I shift and toss, unable to get comfortable with all the bruises from carrying the pack. But it is more than my body that's struggling to adjust. With each subsequent step, the magnitude of this trip—of where caribou might go, of where we might have to follow—impresses itself, leaving me overwhelmed.

The exhilaration of the descent had long since dissipated by morning; in its place came renewed anxiety as we stood at the base of the next ridge. The vertical line that we'd assumed from afar was a drifted-in gully was a caribou trail, and it cut directly up the steepest slope yet. We scanned the long, looming mountainside for another route, and a blank, miles-long wall of snow and rock stared back. Strapping our skis back onto our packs, we slid our hands down our poles and prepared to use them as picks.

Some slopes are a joy to climb, others are agony, and it wasn't long before we'd passed judgment on the one at hand. Our toes hit rock with each kick into the white wall, the thin veneer of snow collapsing underfoot each time we tried to transfer our weight. Step, breathe, step, slip back. Only the occasional plunge into a hidden hole disrupted the rhythm and injected it with a shot of pain. Knees connected with boulders, shins got scraped, elbows bled. I wiped at the sweat pouring into my eyes and waited for Leanne. She passed as I rested, only to rest and be passed. For the next half hour, we swapped leads and curses, wondering why the top wasn't getting any closer.

It was during one of those rest stops that I saw them. I blinked the salt out of my eyes, then blinked again.

"Leanne?" Behind me I heard the stepping and breathing go quiet. "Leanne!"

"Oh my God," she whispered.

A river of caribou was rushing across the valley we'd just traversed, a snaking line of gray backs and churning hooves that turned the snowy trail we'd followed through the sparse trees into an earthy trench. There were thousands of them and more coming, charging across the corrugated landscape below us in an undulating, pulsating, miles-long line.

We were both too stunned to absorb what was happening, too confused to know if it was real or a dream. It was the stuff of picture books, of wildlife films, playing out before us, and if we didn't get moving soon, we would be engulfed, avalanched, or both. Suddenly energized and a little scared, we turned and made a renewed push for the top.

When we crested the ridge, the caribou were piling into the bottom of the slope, the fast-moving line thickening as the leaders slowed and began the steep struggle up. We collapsed on our packs for a few minutes then moved back from the edge, searching for something to hide behind as the animals got close.

"The tent!" Leanne whispered as precious seconds ticked past. Without another word we set it up, grabbed our camera gear, and dove in.

Five minutes passed. Ten. Straining, we listened for the first telltale huffs but heard only our racing hearts. At the fifteen-minute mark, I took a chance and ventured out to peer over the edge. Caribou were strung back across the valley as far as my eye could see, but the leaders had cut a new diagonal line partway up the killer slope. Abandoning the tent, we rushed to a new vantage and hunkered down.

Unlike other members of the deer family, both sexes of caribou grow antlers, and it was the sharp tips of the first cow's rack that announced the beginning of a long procession of caribou heads, caribou bodies, and caribou legs that crested the slope all night. Undetected where we sat 100 yards away, Leanne and I photographed and filmed as they passed, savoring our first close, daylight view of the animals. Larger than deer but smaller than elk or moose, caribou share many characteristics with their southern cousins: long rubbery snouts, cloven hooves (albeit larger and rounder than any of their relatives), and an almost comical pairing of heavily muscled necks, shoulders, and rumps with skinny legs. But these caribou were also noticeably different, seemingly smarter and stronger than the hoofed herbivores I was used to observing farther south. Perhaps it was the ring of dark fur fringing already oversized eyes that gave the impression of a greater awareness, and perhaps it was the sheer number of grunting, prancing animals that inferred greater strength. Whatever it was, there could be no doubt they had tackled the steep climb better than Leanne and I had. Except for the occasional cough or sneeze, there was no hint of shortness of breath and none of the staggering, complaining, or collapsing that had accompanied our own arrival at the top of the slope half an hour before. After less than a minute, every animal was moving again, making room for the legions that came behind.

A mix of age classes passed in front of us—antlerless calves born the year before, spike bulls, and young females—but it was the older cows that made up the majority, crowding the skyline with their sparse antlers, sweeping up and out in thin lines. The big bulls were noticeably absent, staying on the winter range as they did every year, waiting for the snow to melt before following more easily later in the spring. The cows had no such luxury. Even from where we sat, their distended bellies were obvious, urging them northward, pressing against thinly veiled ribs.

It was almost midnight when Leanne and I stole back to the tent and cooked some supper, looking out every few minutes to be sure they still came. They did. We turned off the stove and spooned hot stew into our cold bodies, the muffled sound of hooves and clicking leg tendons murmuring around us like soft rain.

"They're so beautiful," said Leanne.

"They're so skinny," I added, knowing the two are linked: their fragility is part of their grace.

After we'd finished eating, I went outside and stood on the edge of the ridge, on the edge of what seemed to be a very different world, and pulled out my binoculars in the waning light. I looked back at our last campsite, back at our last lunch spot, back at every place we'd rested, and saw caribou connecting all of it, a long thread of animals snaking through the shadows, bringing our past into their present, traveling in an hour what had taken us all day.

I turned, climbed into the tent, and closed my eyes. There could be no doubt: we were in the migration.

The question now was whether we could keep up.

Arctic Ocean

Beaufort Sea

Kaktovik

Herschel
Island

Brooks
Range

Arctic
Village

British
Mtns

Barn
Mtns *Bonnet
Lk*

Aklavik

Inuvik

*Summit
Lk*

Fort
McPherson

Porcupine R

Old
Crow

Yukon R

Fort
Yukon

Fairbanks

NORTHWEST
TERRITORIES

Eagle

Hulahula R

Jago R

Kongakut R

Firth R

Babbage R

Blow R

Bell R

Richardson Mtns

Eagle R

Arctic Circle

100   50   0   100
kilometers

= entire range

= major route

Dawson
City

ALASKA

YUKON

SPRING MIGRATION ROUTES OF THE PORCUPINE CARIBOU HERD

early spring migration

Hunted, then harnessed: isn't this
the sinewy nature of our being?
Path and turning, a touch to guide.
New distances. And the two are one.
        —Rainer Maria Rilke, *Sonnets to Orpheus*, Part One, XI

It was somewhere on the tattered edge of tree line that we saw our first wolf, and when we did, the ribbons of caribou that had been continually surging past us for two days suddenly ceased.

"What's going on?" I wondered aloud as more than a dozen lines of caribou funneled into a V-shaped gully then stopped. They'd been coming for more than an hour, trickling over the ridge we'd camped atop the night before, a net of dark, moving lines covering the white slope we'd descended all morning. But now, backing up above the bottleneck of rock at the bottom of the gully was a reservoir of caribou thousands deep. Leanne set up the tripod and began to film.

"There!" she said, looking through the zoomed-in viewfinder. "To the right."

Using binoculars, I focused on the dot she was looking at: an animal half the size of all the others and 100 yards below the lead caribou, crouched motionless behind some rocks.

"Any others?" I asked, searching the adjoining gullies and hollows for pack mates.

Leanne shook her head.

The seconds ticked past while the wolf remained in position and the mountainside of caribou grew quiet. Even from where we sat watching, more than a mile away, the tension was palpable. Palms sweating and hearts pounding, we waited, stamping warm blood into our feet. After five long minutes, the standoff finally broke.

It took just a fraction of a second for the closest caribou to react to the lunging wolf, and when they did, the entire mountain of animals moved in unison, erupting in a wave of flashing, spinning bodies like a turning, choreographed dance. What had been a stagnant mass of animals suddenly became a single, fleeing organism, and it veered left then right as it surged upward, pulsing silver and black like a school of darting fish. I lowered the binoculars and stood mesmerized by the pattern, watching as 2,000 animals turned back on themselves, rushing for the ridge in a dark cloud of retreat. Columns of snow rose from within the stampeding herd, spreading like a veil behind them, and into it charged a dark smudge that began to close in.

When the wolf was within a few strides of the nearest animals, the blanket of caribou began to unravel from the bottom up. Chasing first one animal and then another, the wolf tried to isolate its victim, but what had started as a straightforward ambush turned into chaos. With the fabric of the herd shredding in all directions, the wolf followed first one thread and then another, hooking left, right, then left again, losing ground with each switch. Indecision led to hesitation, and after a couple of last, desperate lunges, its all-out gallop faltered to a trot.

Leanne and I stood in silence, frozen with awe, as the last of the caribou disappeared over the ridge.

"Can you believe that just happened?" I finally whispered.

But she was too busy to answer, still recording as the wolf lay panting and gulping mouthfuls of snow.

*April 15—Upper reaches of Waters River, Yukon—*In six short days, we have skied and stumbled our way into a river of life, leaving behind the frenetic months of fund-raising, food preparation, and research that typified the winter in Calgary. No traffic jams, no scheduled phone calls, no long nights of letter writing while the brakes of buses and trucks screech outside. In a week, we have traded people for caribou, high-rises for soaring mountains, and a gridlock of streets for winding valleys. There's still pressure, but it's different, surging through instead of gathering within us. No schedules, no timetables, no flashing lights and signs saying which way to go next. It is wolves that tell us when to stop and caribou that urge us forward, pushing and pulling us across this landscape from behind and ahead.

Reluctant to lose our momentum, we pushed hard for the next two days, racing up and down ridges on a widening trail as group after group of caribou passed. Cows, yearlings, and two-year-olds came in surges that were hundreds of animals strong and, after detouring around our hunched-over figures, disappeared into the next valley, up the next mountain, and around the next corner in quickening waves.

"We gotta do something or we're gonna fall behind," I said, watching as yet another band of animals cantered up behind and cut into the soft snow to push around us. We'd detoured only 100 yards away, and we could hear the huffs and grunts of the lead cow from where she churned forward chest-deep while the others followed single-file behind.

"What can we do?" asked Leanne, after they'd rejoined the packed trench and surged off.

I recalled what we'd heard and read about caribou movements before leaving—how a bull had traversed 500 miles in a month, how two cows had wandered 400 miles in three weeks, and how a calf had covered 50 miles a day at two weeks of age—and tried not to despair. The average pace gave us more hope—15 miles a day in spring, summer, and fall—but even that was depressing, considering that we'd failed to cover even half that distance on all but one of the last seven days.

We'd known the trip was going to be tough and, for that very reason, had included a training regime as part of the previous winter's preparations. But with all the meals to get ready and the thousands of dollars to raise, our workouts had given way to the more pressing tasks of writing grant proposals and cooking and drying food. In the end, we'd defaulted to a very different kind of "weight training." Stressed by the way things were going on the financial front and concerned about how little food we were going to be able to carry, we found ourselves opening the fridge and frequenting greasy-spoon diners far more often than usual. By the time we'd hauled ourselves out of Old Crow, we'd each gained 20 pounds.

Now we were paying a price for that lack of physical training, as well as for our widened girths. After a week of yanking ourselves through the trees and plodding to the tops of ridges only to scramble back down again, our bodies had finally gone into shock. I had diarrhea, Leanne was nauseated, and each morning took longer than the last to limber stiff muscles so we could unfold ourselves from the cramped tent.

"I don't know," I said, as another pod of animals took shape on the ridge behind us. "They can't keep coming forever. Sooner or later, something's got to change."

And that afternoon it did. After a week of sunshine, a wall of clouds blew in from the west and snagged on the peaks, plunging us into a world of swirling snowflakes and mist. Hunkering deep into our parka hoods, we pushed on despite the wind and snow, stopping to camp only after the tracks we followed had all but disappeared.

"There're more out there," I reported the next morning after one of my many trips outside.

"More what?"

"Tracks." I said. "Fresh. They must've passed without us hearing."

Ignoring our protesting bodies, we packed up and moved again.

It took only ten minutes to know we'd made a mistake. The caribou too had stopped, and we found them bedded on the ridge in veils of gauzy mist. It was like walking through a stream of illusions; shapes we assumed were boulders suddenly rose and drifted deeper into the clouds. There were no sounds to match the action—the falling snowflakes and thick fog muffled everything—and we moved from one encounter to the next without forewarning. It was thrilling to be so close to the caribou, but we knew it was wrong. Pregnant cow after pregnant cow startled at the sudden sight of us, and on the verge of stumbling into a third group, we stopped, dropped our packs, and pulled out the frozen tent. After traveling a grand total of 500 yards, we resolved to call it a day.

No sooner were we inside the tent, however, than the sound of footsteps had me looking outside. I turned excitedly back to Leanne, already pulling myself from the bag.

"It's clearing and they're moving! Let's go!"

"Moving? How many?"

"Two."

"Two? C'mon, Karst. Give it a rest. You've got the runs; I'm on the way to getting them; we're exhausted, cold, and wet; and you want to pack up just to move a few hundred yards more?"

I looked out as she scolded me, watching as another cloud bank rolled in, wondering if I was obsessed.

Before I could answer my own question, the two cows lay down and began chewing their cud.

When I looked out the tent door the next morning, the storm had washed all the tracks clean, but not much else had changed from the previous days. The sky was clear again, the sun was shining, and scribing across the ridge beside us was another mob of jogging cows. Pausing long enough to gulp down a lukewarm breakfast before setting off after them, we braced ourselves for another discouraging day. But four hours later, after half-skiing and half-falling in a pinball descent into the next narrow valley, we emerged into a different scene.

"We've been spat out of the hills," said Leanne, as the steep walls leaned back and a vast, U-shaped trench opened before us. It was more a wide basin than a valley, fringed on one side by the western flank of the Richardson Mountains and on the other by a series of low bumps that separated it from a prairie of white.

"Still Old Crow Flats?" asked Leanne.

I glanced beyond the bumps to where she pointed. It didn't look anything like the ocean of trees and frozen lakes we'd looked out over just a week before, but it was part of the same endless knot of streams, lakes, and wetlands around which we'd been arcing while following the mountains. There were a few green fingers of forest still jutting north, but the majority of trees had petered out, making it difficult to know what was frozen land and frozen water in the huge, white plain. In the distance, a dark cliff materialized and disappeared in a mirage of heat waves.

"Hot," I said, peeling off a jacket and stuffing it in my pack.

Leanne nodded as she gestured north with an open hand.

"It seems to be slowing the caribou down."

Indeed, the last animals to have passed us earlier that morning could be seen in the distance, a hundred-odd caribou fanned out on the south-facing slopes, feeding on the occasional patch of snow-free ground. Except during the brief storm the night before, this was the first time on the trip that we'd seen caribou stand still.

They didn't stay put for long, however. By the time we'd covered half of the 2 miles separating us, they were moving again—but only as far as the next island of melted-off grass. Happy they hadn't gone far, we skirted around them, finding our own knoll of snow-free tundra to camp on, only to have the caribou climb down and, in turn, slip past us. Here, they didn't have to churn through soft snow to get around us. Open, treeless, and scoured by a winter's worth of wind, what was underfoot was as hard as concrete. There were no huffs as the caribou passed, no grunts, just the soft click of tendons ticking like hundreds of clocks as we dropped off to sleep.

The wide Driftwood River valley, along with sunlight growing warm enough to melt snow during the peak of the afternoons, was the perfect setting for a game that unfolded between us and the caribou over the next two days. Or, more accurately, two games: a tortoise-and-hare-type chase, played out as a giant version of connect-the-dots. The dots were snow-free patches of lichen and sedges; the hares were the caribou moving between the dots. The tortoises were us.

So many of the caribou looked alike that it was impossible to say who was gaining and who was falling behind, the tortoises or the hares. Just when I thought I'd identified a unique cow from the day before—with a broken-off antler, for example—another would appear that looked exactly the same. But it didn't matter. Compared to the rush that had consumed us in the mountains, just being among caribou without the soft snow and trees to bog us down was enough. Our packs were getting lighter, our muscles were stronger, and we were covering twice as many miles with half the effort. Despite the fear I'd had while looking down from the airplane, we were moving into the white nothingness with relative ease.

More comfortable and better rested than I'd felt since we'd started, I looked back on the puzzle of caribou behavior and suddenly realized how it all fit. Of course the caribou had rushed through the mountains. They had to: it was the transition zone between where they could dig for food (in the sheltered forests below tree line) and where they wouldn't have to dig at all (the windswept, sun-baked slopes flanking Old Crow Flats). And of course they'd had impeccable timing. If they'd arrived a week earlier, the sun wouldn't have had the energy to melt off the concretelike layer of snow covering their food, and if they'd waited longer, they would have spent valuable energy wallowing in the same deep, soft snow they'd endured all winter. Instead, they were capitalizing on the delicate balance between winter wind and spring sun.

I shared my realization with Leanne as we admired another evening procession of animals plodding past our tent in parallel lines. Behind them, a flock of ptarmigans lifted out of a clump of willows, leaving a trail of white feathers hanging in the breeze.

"So you think the rush is over?" she asked, after absorbing what I'd said. "You think this is one of those migrations that drifts instead of races to the Arctic coast?"

She was talking about a rare trend we'd found embedded in the maps and statistics about the spring migration: every few years, when conditions were perfect and they'd left their wintering grounds early, the caribou meandered more than hurried to their calving grounds.

It was exactly what I was thinking, but I didn't dare admit it for fear of how premature it might sound.

Had another wolf not arrived, the peaceful state we'd happened upon in the Driftwood valley might have lasted indefinitely. Later that evening, however, a lanky gray animal slunk out of a shadowy draw, and every feeding, resting caribou within sight came alert.

It wasn't the same wolf we'd seen before—this one was much larger and lighter colored—and this time we weren't watching from a mile away. Camped on a rib of rock that rose a few hundred feet from the valley floor, we were like a couple of eagles perched on a midstream boulder, watching currents of predator and prey about to collide. Along one side of the rock rib walked the wolf, on the other waited the caribou, 400 yards apart in a standoff that was about to explode.

The wolf didn't hurry into the chase. Careful not to look right at the caribou, it angled toward them, its late-evening shadow contracting and expanding like a dark spirit as it padded across the snowdrifts. Hitting our ski tracks on its casual, oblique line, it stopped for a moment, sniffed, then looped away, approaching twice more before mustering the courage to hop across the double set of strange, parallel trails. When it did, the closest group of caribou took a perfectly coordinated step back.

The wolf got within 300 yards of the vigilant, waiting animals then stopped and sniffed the wind. Almost four hundred caribou had bunched together by then, and the sound of stomping feet and snorting animals drifted up and over us like a building wave of applause. The wolf took two more steps forward, stopped and sniffed again, then looked up and down the line.

"Here we go," I whispered.

Leanne swung around from where she sat hunched over the film equipment and told me to hush. By the time she turned back, the chase was on.

Sitting much closer than we had to the last hunt, I was struck most by the noise as the caribou took off—hooves pounding hard snow like hail pelting a quiet lake. But soon it was the patterns that once again had me mesmerized: lines of caribou bunching into larger and larger clumps until the herd moved like a giant inkblot, seeming to float more than flee, drifting farther into a checkerboard of shadow and light.

I didn't think the wolf had much chance of succeeding when it first took off, but what it lacked in speed it made up for in endurance.

Breaking through the crust every third or fourth stride, it pursued far into the distance, neither gaining nor losing ground until it was more than a mile away. Then, with a few of the weaker caribou tiring, it began to close in.

The whole group of caribou surged in a last-minute burst of speed, but it was no use. Seconds later the gray wolf was into the back of the herd, breaking it apart, isolating a victim. A few of the stragglers veered from the main group and the wolf followed, honing in on a tired youngster moving a step slower than the rest. The young caribou, not quite a year old, swerved once, stumbled, and, when something roared into its flank, spun to face its demise. Pouncing, the wolf yanked at its neck, and the two animals crashed into the snow, locked together as half a dozen convulsions ensued.

For the next few minutes, the other caribou continued to run, tracing a broad circle that eventually brought them to a standstill just 100 yards from the panting wolf. Hooves pranced and legs stamped as they rid themselves of their adrenaline, then they stood quiet again, alert, waiting, watching just as before. But it was the end of the chase, not the beginning, and with one caribou dead, there was no reason for the dance between predator and prey to resume just yet. The wolf turned to the carcass, ignoring the line of caribou, and the caribou, in turn, filed 100 yards behind the wolf as they pushed forward on their unstoppable journey north.

Lack of food, not the wolf, brought an end to the flow we'd enjoyed with the caribou. A day later, after we'd resumed the pattern of passing animals only to be passed, we reached into our food bag and the reality of our situation set in.

"One, maybe two days is all we have left," said Leanne, passing me the dregs of a few broken crackers and the last handful of nuts. After a snack that left me grossly unsatisfied, I dug out the satellite phone, extended the antennae, and made the call.

The days of packaging all our food caches before flying to Old Crow had been harried. After making the five-day drive north from Calgary with only one breakdown, we'd taken over the Parks Canada warehouse in Inuvik, unloaded the boxes that filled the back of our rusted old pickup, and started to sort, mark, and repackage 180 days' worth of dried food. Fruit bars, boxes of nuts and raisins, blocks of cheese, and bags of oats, cornmeal, granola, and milk powder were soon scattered across the plywood floor of the giant metal building, and on every available shelf sat a multitude of dinners we'd cooked and dried ourselves: shrimp green curry, chicken almond rice, bison basil tomato sauce, macaroni and cheese. Using a mix of donated and discounted ingredients, we'd scratched together a respectable seven-day menu, and we set about organizing it into thirteen caches of two weeks' worth of meals each.

At the peak of packaging, we'd covered the whole warehouse, but through a back-to-back stint of two long days and even longer nights, we got the supplies organized. After adding cooking fuel, camera film, videotapes, a small tube of toothpaste, sunscreen, and boot grease to each pile, I'd begun taping the first package into a large ball when Leanne walked up with a smile.

"Don't forget a few of these," she said, holding some condoms in her fingers.

"I guess it is our honeymoon," I laughed, squeezing them in through a crack before wrapping the whole package with crushed newspaper and a final layer of tape. In the midst of all the planning, fund-raising, and preparations of the previous fall and winter, we'd found the time to get married. Whether or not we would have the time and energy to celebrate it during the trip remained to be seen.

"Whaddya think?" I asked, climbing on top of a stepladder before tossing the padded ball to the floor.

Leanne winced as it hit with a thud. "Better to have the plane land than throw it."

"Yeah," I'd agreed. "As long as we have the choice."

On that first resupply, we did have a choice. After hanging up the phone, I pulled out the map and pointed to a blue dot 10 miles away, just beyond the low pass at the head of the Driftwood River.

"The pilot says he can probably land on the ice at Bonnet Lake. Figures he can come tomorrow if the weather holds."

Leanne looked up at the blue sky as I said it, then back down at the map and smiled. Everything was lining up perfectly: the half-mile-wide body of water sat right along the northwest trajectory the caribou had been following for the last four days. It was farther from the mountains—out in the low hills that sat between the Richardsons and the Barn Range—but the caribou would need to cross between those chains sooner or later, and if all our predictions were right, they would probably go right past Bonnet Lake when they did.

Everything unfolded as we'd expected for the rest of the morning, and the view from the top of the last of the many knolls we'd climbed and camped on during our long, gradual ascent of the Driftwood River led us to believe that it was also going to be a straightforward afternoon. Trending over the low ridge ahead was a well-trod caribou trail in exactly the direction we wanted. The only problem was that in front of it, right where the knoll and surrounding hills created the only real bottleneck in the entire valley, lay a group of sleeping caribou.

"This time I guess we have to wait," I said, settling into the rocks. Leanne sat beside me, huddling out of the wind. The sky stretched blue above us, but the breeze had swung out of the north, and it brought a midday bite that had us donning down jackets and pulling our neck tubes halfway up our faces.

"A lot of creatures have seen a lot of things from here," mumbled Leanne from behind her veil of polar fleece. Farther back along the rocky knoll, we'd found owl castings littering the high points and wolf tracks pressed in the snow all around us. As we waited for the caribou to move, a pair of gyrfalcons swooped between the two rock outcrops that protruded from the gravel, calling in shrill screams. I scanned the caves and crevices for their nest, half expecting to find evidence of a nomadic people—arrowheads and spear points from Randall's great-grandfather, perhaps—but found only animal droppings in the hollows and overhangs where the rock had been polished smooth. Nonetheless, when I turned back to look at the caribou, I sensed that mine weren't the first human eyes to have looked down on that very scene.

"They're moving," I said to Leanne as first one and then another animal got up, took a few tentative steps toward the well-worn trail, then waited for another to follow. It was a start-up-and-go routine we'd watched many times before, one that sometimes took hours, and I settled back to watch as another animal got up and the original pair repeated the routine, trying to recruit enough individuals to unseat the inertia that had gripped the herd.

It was just as the threshold seemed to be reached, just when half the group was up and walking, that a raven flew overhead, called out twice, and everything changed. A lone cow near the back of the group started off in another direction, two others followed after it, and the original leader stopped to size up the renegades who, in turn, halted to look back at her. Every animal ceased moving in that moment, and then the indecision broke. The leaders became followers, and the whole group set off on a new path, heading northeast instead of northwest.

"This can't be happening," cried Leanne—but it was. After two weeks of hard effort to find and follow caribou, now we were forced to abandon them to meet our human needs.

We weren't far down the old trail when we discovered the reason the latest group of caribou hadn't followed all the others. After cresting the first rise, we spotted five dark circles tucked into the hollows of a drifted-in creek. I pulled out the binoculars and turned to Leanne as she skied up beside me:

"Wolves," I said. "A pack of them. Sleeping."

We were downwind and 300 yards away, but again the raven flew overhead and again it cawed. In an instant the wolves were up and running, their fleeing bodies no longer the quiet, relaxed bundles they'd been a moment before. We watched as one gray, one brown, and three black animals grappled up the side of the ravine and broke into the open, their legs cycling hard to widen the distance between where they ran and where we stood.

I had heard plenty of wolves howl while I'd worked as a park warden and biologist, but none was like the sound that came from the largest animal when it stopped, threw back its head, and shrieked. It was a call of indignation, of fearful anger, and when another stopped and joined in, Leanne and I dropped to our knees. Staring through us, the two then turned and ran after the others, their thick coats ruffling in the wind. They stood out from the landscape, yet fit perfectly in it, black and gray shadows streaking across the white drifts—but something was amiss. A calm confidence known only by those creatures found at the top of the food chain had been violated, and it would take days, if not weeks, for the outrage we'd inflicted to fade. As we set off again, we felt very upright, very obtuse. Very human.

What we found at the bottom of the snowy ravine was a shock but no surprise. Scattered among the round depressions where the wolves had slept were spatters of blood-stained snow, pieces of caribou hide, and large packed-down areas strewn with pink bones.

"They've been down here for weeks," said Leanne as we stood deep within the chasm of steep cutbanks and overhanging drifts. I nodded, looking where all the paths padded by paws intersected those trampled by hooves. It was the perfect ambush, and we had ruined all of it, abetted by the raven that had first warned the caribou about the wolves and then the wolves about us. Of all the players, we seemed to be the only ones who hadn't understood.

The wolves were still running, barely visible, when we climbed out the other side of the ravine and continued on the old trail. They were running full speed, dots heading straight for the line of caribou we'd abandoned, and I worried their approach would turn the caribou even farther away from Bonnet Lake. But in a strange twist I never expected, the two adversaries crossed paths within yards of one another without altering their respective directions or speed. The wolves kept galloping southwest up the mountainside, and the caribou happily plodded along the valley, continuing northeast.

We followed the old trail to the crest of a low ridge, then stopped before descending into the wide, rolling basin where Bonnet Lake sat hidden in a fold some 8 or 9 miles away. The place where we stood was an edge of sorts, the beginning of an open, rolling transition zone that hung like a giant saddle between the Richardson and Barn mountains. But it was more than geography that was changing. Clouds were rolling in, and after we'd followed caribou past rock towers and sunlit peaks for the past week, it felt wrong to be heading alone into a windswept basin of murky horizons and look-alike hills. There were no animals coming up the trail behind us, and the old hoofprints we were following were already fading in the drifts forming ahead of the incoming storm.

And yet we had to keep going, for despite the belonging we'd started to feel among the caribou, we were still human, still hungry, and still dependent on a resupply from the outside world.

If we'd wanted a spot to wait out bad weather, Bonnet Lake didn't fit the bill. Situated at the low point between mountain chains, it, along with the nearby Blow River valley, formed the squeeze point where cold coastal and warm interior air masses mixed. To the south lay Old Crow Flats, to the north was the Arctic Ocean, and between the two we found the wind-polished surface of frozen Bonnet Lake.

When we first saw the roofs of three small buildings poking over the horizon, we were hopeful, but with each subsequent stride the reality of their true condition set in. They were doorless, windowless, and, in some cases, wall-less husks of a former exploration and research camp, and in the decades since the prospectors, biologists, and others had left, the bears, rodents, and snow had moved in.

"I wouldn't want to be here when the grizzlies come out of hibernation," I said, tugging at one of the many clumps of blond hair crimped in the door and window frames. Leanne scanned the bite and claw marks on the outside walls then peered through one of the gaping holes.

"Drifts right up to the ceiling," she said as a gust of wind swirled around her. "I can't even step in." As all hope of an alternative shelter vanished, we unpacked the tent yet again.

The brewing storm hadn't quite hit when the plane arrived late the next morning, but it wasn't far off. Dropping through a hole in the thickening clouds, the pilot veered as another wave of snow blew across the lake, then he set the skis down hard.

"Hold this," he barked, tossing me a rope before easing off on the throttle. No sooner had I grabbed the braided nylon strands than the plane's tail slapped around in the wind.

"Got it?" he shouted, swiping at his baseball cap as it threatened to lift from his balding head.

Nodding, I tightened my grip.

"I won't be staying to chat," he explained after motioning to the dark horizon. He looked up after dropping our two boxes on the ice. "Have you got anything to go out?"

Leanne ran to the tent and fetched twelve days' worth of exposed film and videotape and nonburnable garbage.

"That's it?"

"That's it."

Not wasting a moment, he climbed back into the cockpit, gunned the engine, and nodded for me to let go. "Whatever it is you're doing out here, good luck!"

I opened my mouth, but just as I started to answer a gust slammed his door shut. Ten seconds later, he was gone.

I can't recall why we ignored the worsening weather and decided to pack up. Perhaps it was the thought of having to lie awake as the decrepit shacks flapped and groaned around us for another long night. Or maybe it was our desire to be with caribou—or just the simple human belief that it is always better somewhere else. Regardless of the reason, after a half hour of stuffing our new supplies into our packs, we lit up the leftover boxes, clipped on our skis, and set off leaning sideways as a trail of flames and ashes tumbled down the lake.

We expected to have to backtrack at least 5 miles before finding any sign of caribou, but only ten minutes later a strange resistance underfoot made me look down.

"Brown ski wax!" I shouted, but the wind stole the joke before it reached Leanne's ears. I tapped on her hood as she pulled up beside me, then pointed down to the fresh scat. No sooner had she seen the dark pellets than another wave of snow washed over them, also obscuring our feet.

"Keep going?" I asked when her goggled face looked back at me.

"We've started now," she shouted back. Pulling up our neck tubes, we inched deeper into the storm.

What the wind took away from visibility it revealed in textures. Cutting away the soft snow around the hard-packed hoofprints, it left a trail of protruding tracks, and we made our way along it, feeling more than seeing. The Braille-like approach worked, but when a powerful gust toppled me over fifteen minutes later, I knew the folly had to end. Reaching into the storm, I pulled Leanne's cloaked head next to mine and shouted where I thought her ear would be. We had to stop.

We'd deliberated a long time over what kind of tent to bring on the trip, and right then I was thankful we'd opted for a custom model made for high-altitude climbers. It wasn't a high peak we were aspiring to scale—just keeping pace with pregnant caribou—but the conditions were no different. Together we pulled it out of Leanne's pack, pounced on it before it blew away, then crawled inside the envelope of fabric to wrestle with the poles from within. Once it was set up, we hauled in our packs and breathed a sigh of relief. We had shelter. We had food again. We were safe.

But soon the wind was challenging that notion. Within minutes the poles were bending at angles I never would've thought possible, lying flat only to pop up again while the walls flapped and heaved like a giant, hyperventilating lung.

"Do you think it'll hold?" I asked, but no sooner had Leanne started to answer than I was diving for the far corner, pushing the lifting floor back to the ground. Another wall of pressure came and went, a shower of ice crystals bore through the fabric, and then a low moan filled the momentary silence that came afterward, announcing the next incoming wave of wind.

We spent the next half hour with our backs braced against the north wall, our muscles tensing and releasing with each gust and lull. Blast after blast hit, and as the spindrift came through the zippers, I inspected and reinspected every stitch and seam. I thought of the workers in the factory the day we'd picked up the tent, of the thickness of the thread spooled on their heavy machines, and wondered if any of them ever thought of their sewing as having the potential to save someone's life.

After an hour without the tent shredding around us, we let go of the poles long enough to peel off our wet clothes and climb into the damp sleeping bag. Then we grabbed hold of the poles again, feeling the vibration and energy of the storm travel through our fingertips, down our arms, and into our shuddering bodies. There was no sleeping, no eating, drinking, or even talking. Like the drifts in the shacks we'd left that morning, the storm moved into every corner of the tent and our bodies, leaving no room for even a thought.

When one of the skis anchoring the tent's guy lines popped out of the snow, I knew I had to go outside. Leaving Leanne to brace the poles on her own, I piled on every bit of my clothing, then muscled my way out the door.

For the first few seconds I just knelt there, trying to adjust to a world that had been rubbed white. Everything was gone, replaced by wind-driven snow: our skis, our poles, our tracks—even the tent was caked and rimed with ice. I looked down and watched as the color of my jacket and pants began to fade and disappear. If I didn't hurry, the blizzard was going to erase me as well.

After ramming the ski back into the snow, I set about building a snow wall upwind of the tent. I needed a knife, not the soft aluminum blade of the shovel that bent each time I stabbed at the hard drifts, but after I pushed and sliced an inch at a time, a chunk of rocklike snow broke free. One brick, and then another. I shuttled from wall to quarry as the snow continued to swirl around me, and the wedge gradually took form.

Not until I was done did I look up, and that's when I saw them: half a dozen gray shapes filtering in and out of the clouds, smudges of charcoal in swirls of white flakes. Squinting harder, I tried to make out whether they were rocks, shrubs, or something else. The wind eased for a moment, the curtain of snow dropped, and in the second of calm before another veil was lifted, I knew what the shapes were.

"Caribou!" I cheered as I dove back inside the tent.

Eyes closed and hands still clasped to the poles, Leanne looked as though she'd been crucified by the storm.

"Yeah right," she shivered, but with a little prodding she agreed to look.

"Caribou!" she confirmed once she'd poked her head out the door. "Dozens." Pulling on frozen clothes, she grabbed her camera and headed outside.

> *April 22—Headwaters of the Blow River, Yukon*—The caribou are an island of calm in the raging blizzard, feeding, resting—even chewing their cud—while the wind hurls past in waves of horizontal snow. The sky is still dark, the ice crystals bore into us like bullets, but after watching the animals go about their business, our panic fades. Without shelter or even food, they are comfortable, making our own worries laughable. The poles still flex, the tent still pops, but instead of a life-or-death situation, the caribou remind us, it is just another day.

Leanne walked past, barefoot, in underwear and tee shirt, carrying a handful of dirty socks. Laundry day. I rolled onto my stomach and watched as a spider crawled through a mat of dry leaves, disappearing under my glistening bare arm. Forty-eight hours since we'd almost frozen to death, and now I was sweating. Leanne caught my lazy look as she leaned over the pot of hot water and smiled back. We'd stopped asking each other hours ago, but the question still hung in the warm air between us: how could this be the same place?

When the storm had finally cleared, we'd rushed to get across the Blow River, following dark curving lines of caribou that had seemed as keen as we'd been to flee that reviled valley. But we needn't have hurried. Now not a cloud was in the sky, and as I looked back from where we sat on the eastern edge of the Barn Range, it was columns of heat, not walls of snow, that obscured the view. In the span of a single day, the temperature had climbed 30 degrees Fahrenheit.

The warm weather made camping comfortable, but it also brought new problems. Nothing we used when we set off the next morning— not wax, klister, or paraffin—prevented the wet, sticky snow from globbing to the bottoms of our skis—and with each passing hour, those places that still held snow became fewer and farther between. It made for difficult skiing and difficult tracking: instead of following long, continuous trenches of snowy hoofprints, we found ourselves following fragments of trails, a set of tracks across a drift here, a few marks in a snowy gully there, with no sense of what had happened on the growing patches of bare ground between.

It didn't help that the caribou had dispersed as soon as we'd hit the Barn Mountains. No sooner had we climbed out of the wide, flat trench of the Blow River valley than the groups we'd followed for two weeks began to scatter and spread out. We'd chosen to follow a valley somewhere in the middle of the corrugated line of cone-shaped peaks, but it could just as easily have been any other in the multitude of V-shaped clefts and folds that drained into the larger Blow River. A few caribou had gone up each one of them, the tight lines and dark masses of previous weeks spreading into a shotgun pattern of disappearing dots.

The mountains we found to the west of the storm were warmer, less rugged, and more convoluted than the Richardsons: a thin band of peaks with just as many angles, alcoves, and valleys, but squeezed into a much smaller space. Switching from walking to skiing to walking again, we climbed past the first blooms of purple saxifrage on bare ridge tops, dropped down to where the furry beginnings of pussy willows lined still-frozen creeks, and camped in the tight, windless valleys, confident that if another storm came, we'd survive.

Despite their sheltered feeling, the Barn Mountains were incredibly lonely. A few ptarmigans called from where they stayed hidden in the willows, and we spotted half a dozen scattered caribou, but the rest of our searches of the mottled, browning landscape ended in vain. Our days of connecting the dots with caribou had turned into a lonely snow-patch hopscotch, and after two more days of searching, we couldn't help but wonder what our roles were in the new game they were playing.

"Could we have moved ahead?" Leanne asked a few evenings later. I sat in the tent beside her, studying the map while she kneeled over the first-aid kit and tended to her hands. They were a testament to the extremes we'd already endured—a rash of sun blisters across the backs; red, swollen, and frostnipped on the tips of her fingers—and I winced as she pierced the largest lesion with a sterile needle, draining the pus.

"I don't know what to think," I admitted, looking away. We still hadn't seen more than a few dozen caribou, all of which were pairs, trios, and lone individuals that scarcely seemed to move. Perhaps we were moving ahead, or perhaps we had fallen behind. For all I knew, we were on the slow margins of a herd that thundered onward, hidden just a valley or two away.

"Well, what does the report say?" she asked, fiddling with a bandage.

The report was *The Status and Life History of the Porcupine Caribou Herd*, published in 1986 by the Yukon government, that I'd photocopied, shrunk, and pasted inside the cover of my journal before leaving. It was a little outdated, but its description of the overall movements of the herd was among the better and more concise summaries we'd found during our research. I turned to the back of my notebook and began to read.

"It says here the route of the spring migration is 'highly variable among years,'" I began.

Leanne frowned. "What else?"

"It talks about four major corridors during the spring migration. One follows the Richardson Mountains then turns northwest into the Barn Range."

"We've done that," Leanne said with a hint of impatience. "But the Barn Range is 50 miles wide. Anything more specific?"

I shook my head as I searched the text, trying not to let the frequency of words such as "appears," "may," and "sometimes" get me down. The lack of concrete information hadn't been lost on the author. A well-known Yukon biologist with a reputation for creative thinking, he had gone far beyond the boundaries of technical writing to summarize the situation.

"Listen," I said, smiling as I read out loud:

> The migrating herd can be imagined as a giant amoeba gradually shifting its mass northward by a process that entails the rapid streaming of cytoplasm (caribou) in some sections, while elsewhere the cytoplasm is hardly moving at all or is slowly flowing in different directions. Yet the overall effect is one of a coordinated reorganization that eventually transfers the cell (Porcupine herd) to a position along the coastal regions of the Yukon and northeast Alaska. Each spring this shift occurs in a unique combination of cytoplasmic withdrawals and amalgamations but always produces a similar distribution by early June.

Leanne laughed as I closed the notebook. "Pretty good description of the indescribable."

I nodded as I pored over the map, no more enlightened than before. Worried about what was happening, I looked back at the route we'd covered, searching for a hint of what might happen next. But there were no patterns, no trends to hang the future on: big groups to no groups; rushing to resting; cold to hot; blizzard to calm. The only thing that hadn't changed was change itself.

Using the edge of my compass against the map, I made a few measurements and ran through dates in my head.

"You know, if this continues—if the caribou keep spreading out and we can't track them—we may have to head for the calving grounds without them."

Leanne's face went serious as she looked up from putting everything back into the first-aid kit. We'd talked about such a possibility before we'd started the trip, of adopting an "approximate" migratory path if we lost the caribou, but it wasn't a plan either of us liked.

"We have another five weeks before they'll start calving. How far is the Alaskan coastal plain?"

"About 300 miles," I answered.

Leanne nodded, trying not to show her disappointment. After overcoming months of uncertainty to find and travel with caribou, we now risked losing not only the animals but the flow we'd felt alongside them in the Driftwood valley and the inspiration they'd brought during the storm. To now set our own schedule, route, and destination independent of the animals seemed shallow and trite.

Our goal was to be caribou, not human. The last thing either of us wanted was to turn what had started as a very special journey into just another cross-country hiking trip.

late spring migration

Pure attention, the essence of the powers!
Distracted by each day's doing,
how can we hear the signals?
— Rainer Maria Rilke, *Sonnets to Orpheus,* Part One, XII

The Canoe River had stalled the caribou, but it was more than flowing water and creaking panes of ice that troubled them. Too many sightlines were cut short in the narrow, twisting valley, and the animals near the back of the group were as unsettled as those pawing at the shore. When a ptarmigan flushed from a nearby patch of willows, the nearest cow jumped, turning every animal back on the one behind it in a stampeding retreat. But no sooner were they off than they stopped again, torn with desire and fear as they looked back toward the opposite shore. Their breathing quieted, rolled-back eyes slid forward, and after a period of milling, the animals drifted back to the riverbank, looking for something new in a crossing that hadn't changed.

After a few more minutes of indecision, two of the lead animals crept to the edge, nosed the soft ice, and, with all eyes watching, took a skating step in. Water lapped at their hooves as they stood there, then rose to their shins as they slid forward, but in the same moment they tried to back out, the rest of the herd surged from behind and all but pushed them in.

Because Arctic rivers and creeks freeze solid in winter and then melt from the top down, a spring crossing that looks deep and dangerous to a southerner is usually nothing more than a shallow-water crossing on submerged ice that's still many feet thick. Usually. Patterns of freeze-up, the presence of springs or air pockets, and the length of time and speed at which the water has been running all complicate the situation. Four legs or two, though, the risks are essentially the same.

This particular crossing wasn't nearly as deep or dramatic as the ones I'd watched in previous years on the Firth River, nor was it anything like the film footage I'd seen of hundreds of animals dying when the Porcupine River had become a conveyor belt of churning ice. But there was a haunting similarity to all of them, a critical point where, no matter the consequences, a group decision was made and there was no turning back. No sooner were the two lead scouts plunging up to their knees through the water than every animal was in motion, individual trepidation switching to group bravery as they charged forward, three abreast.

It was as if a floodgate had opened, and for the next few minutes Leanne and I photographed the surge of brown bodies that splashed across the blue-green river as we tried to capture the rush of animals in a rainbow of water, slush, and splintered ice. When the last caribou was across, we climbed out from behind the drift where we'd been hiding and looked where they gathered 300 yards beyond the opposite shore. They were grazing; a palpable ease replaced the tension. Unseen predators and poor ice hadn't materialized. Another hurdle had passed.

"Our turn," I said, walking to the river as I rolled long underwear and pants up over my knees. Pulling off my boots, I tied them, my socks, and the skis to my pack and hoisted it all over a shoulder.

After I stumbled barefoot a few steps across snow and sharp rocks, it was almost a relief to slide onto the flat ice. But then the cold set in. Sole-numbing cold crept up into my ankles, turning my lower legs into wooden stumps. Using my poles like crutches, I made my way across the brisk current, seeing but not feeling the water rise over my knees. Apart from an occasional slipperiness, I had no sense that it was ice underfoot, not gravel or rocks.

I wanted to make the crossing look easy for Leanne's sake, to show little pain or discomfort, but when the ice shelf on the far side collapsed beneath me, the composure I'd worked so hard to maintain vanished. Screaming, I bolted for the nearest patch of bare ground, breaking through the ice every second and third step in a trail of blood and shredded skin. When I reached the shore, I rolled onto my back and shook my cut feet skyward, howling as the pain worsened in the biting wind.

Leanne did better, not in terms of wounds she sustained but in how she managed the pain. She too broke through the ice after climbing out of the cold water, but instead of screaming as the shards sliced her legs and feet, she silently bit her lip. Only after collapsing beside me did she start cursing and crying. Having pulled socks and boots back on, I joined her as the feeling began to return to my feet in a sadistic flush of heat.

We were still yammering and swinging our legs when another wave of animals came into view, shouldering around the hill a little higher than the others, charging for the very crossing we'd just made. Scrambling to gather our belongings, we bolted 50 yards, hunkered behind some bushes, and forgot the pain. We were too busy with cameras and lenses, too entranced as the galloping caribou set a drifted-in gully into a dozen tiny avalanches, too excited with the anticipation of what was about to unfold again. Focusing my camera on the spot where caribou and humans had just crossed, I waited for more caribou to enter the frame.

Not since the Richardson Mountains had we seen such life, and as I watched a stream of legs caper through ice and water, I couldn't help but feel we were back in the migration. These were no lone animals but tight-knit, rushing groups, and as they passed and drifted out of sight I found myself looking over my shoulder for the rest of the afternoon.

But no more came. Not in the Canoe valley that day, not at the Babbage River the day after, nor in the Trail or Tuluqaq rivers we waded three days later. The Barn Range peters into hills by that point, and those hills gradually increase in elevation until they merge into the British Mountains of Ivvavik National Park. But there were only caribou trails from years past on the rocky slopes all around, trails that disappeared beneath scattered snow patches and melting drifts.

Moving faster on skis than on foot, we stuck to those patches and drifts wherever possible, winding from shadow to hollow, detouring widely to avoid the hummocky, bumpy tundra that is so awkward on foot. When the snow did run out, we simply kept going with our skis on, bridging trenches that would have gobbled our boots whole.

"Wonder how the ski areas would describe these conditions?" I asked as a thick layer of grass accumulated on the sticky undersides of my skis.

"Let me see," Leanne pondered, poking at the ground with a pole. "Soft-packed in the moguls; watch for hazards in the open; and excellent skiing in the trees?"

"There are no trees," I laughed.

Leanne glanced back as she kept poling across the dry tundra. "Did you want a ski report, or did you want the truth?"

Even though we weren't with the herd and instead followed an average migratory path, we found ourselves in good humor. Ten days had passed since we'd left Bonnet Lake, twenty-seven since we'd parted company with James and Randall, and we'd reached a point on the trip where the pain of starting out had all but faded away. The blisters had gone down, soft muscles had hardened, and the camping, cooking, and packing that had consumed so much effort at the start of the trip became nothing more than a comfortable routine at the beginning and end of each rhythmical day. We weren't moving *with* caribou, but we were moving *like* caribou: simply, efficiently, and fast, defaulting to the path of least resistance even when it was a curving, indirect line.

But contentment never stayed long, and no sooner had we found ease in movement than new worries and discomforts crowded in. The weather worsened; concerns about crossing the Firth dominated our thoughts as we drew close to the big river; and we were suddenly gripped by a hunger that wouldn't quit. We went to bed hungry, woke up hungry, and felt as hungry after breakfast, lunch, and dinner as before each scant meal.

We'd known from the beginning that we couldn't possibly carry enough food to replace the calories we'd need to follow the caribou, and now that we were a month into the trip, we realized the weight we'd gained beforehand wasn't enough. Leanne's little potbelly was shrinking and my fat cheeks were hollowing, and as the temperatures turned cold again, the mornings became tough to endure. Instead of getting up early to beat the heat, we now huddled in the sleeping bag waiting for warmth that never came.

It was no blizzard—the wind was light, but when it swung out of the north, the moisture-laden air off the Arctic Ocean was cold and damp, and it lingered around the pass where we'd been forced to camp in a heavy blanket of fog and snow. The few ground squirrels we'd seen on the surrounding hillsides disappeared into their burrows, the roosterlike ptarmigans in the valley below quieted, and the world was white again.

This time, no caribou walked out of the mist to inspire us, which left me little choice but to revert to my more human tendency: to scheme my way out of a predicament rather than wait and see what would happen next. Pulling out the maps, I refined our so-called migratory route and pushed it farther north than we'd originally planned, making it so we'd cross the Firth River at a place I knew well.

"Cabin?" asked Leanne.

"Yeah, you know, the one where Steve and I first saw the herd," I explained, telling her how the old Canadian Water Survey station would solve all our problems: shelter from the weather, a good place to receive a food drop, and, on the side of the river closest to us, an instrument shed with an old rubber dinghy stored inside. "Beds with mattresses; forks, knives, and plates; four sturdy walls and a solid roof; room to have a sponge bath . . ."

Leanne held up her hand. Sweaty and smelly from a month of hard living, she needed no convincing. After digging through my pack, she handed me the satellite phone.

When a park warden answered and said they were getting ready to leave on their annual spring snowmobile patrol into the park, I couldn't believe my ears. Yes, they could bring in our food, he said, and yes, he thought the dinghy was still in the shack. If all went according to plan, everything would be waiting for us in two days.

"Anything else?" he asked before I hung up.

"Pardon me?"

"Do you want us to bring anything else?"

My mouth began to water. Leanne and I had gone to considerable effort to include only the highest-quality ingredients in our food caches—organically grown and homemade meals as much as possible—but with my stomach grumbling, all concerns over health and nutrition suddenly vanished.

"Anything greasy or sweet."

The next two days were a trudge: up and over a pass obscured in heavy fog, then more clouds as we dropped into the next narrow valley, battling a headwind the whole way down. With the bit of new snow that had fallen, the skiing was better than it had been in more than a week, but I failed to really notice, for without caribou around to hold my attention, my mind wandered to places not visited for a very long time. I don't know whether it was the slide-and-glide rhythm of skiing, the month of wilderness immersion, or both that were reponsible, but something was happening inside my head—a cleanse of sorts, as though the damper that held down useless memories, thoughts, and information had lifted and the long-overdue mental purge had begun: Old phone numbers and addresses came out of nowhere, alongside birthdays of long-lost schoolmates. And, of course, the songs.

"What *are* you singing?" asked Leanne after a few hours of plodding. She stopped so suddenly that my ski tips ran over the back of her skis.

I snapped back to the moment. "Singing?"

"Yeah, you know, humming with words."

I stalled for a few seconds, a little embarrassed. It wasn't conscious. Words to songs I'd never sung before were passing across my lips.

"Oh, that," I cringed. "REO Speedwagon."

"REO Speedwagon?! Are you kidding me? That eighties crap?"

I didn't bother defending myself, hoping she'd forget about it.

"What about before that?"

"What?"

"Before that," Leanne pressed. "You were singing something else." She whistled the first few notes, knowing full well what it was.

"Men at Work," I confessed.

"I knew it! More oldies junk! Would you just stop it? I'm humming it now too and it's driving me nuts!"

I kept my mouth shut, following her ski track as more old songs rattled through my head.

What finally pushed the last of the old lyrics out of my mind and pulled me back into the present were grizzly bear tracks, a set of staggered prints I skied over before I saw them—and not because they were too small to notice. Measuring twice as wide as my hand and longer than my ski boot, each print was capped with a quintet of holes made by 4-inch-long claws. The tracks were old—frozen and thawed a few times over—but I stopped and glassed everything within view anyway, my heart thumping in my ears.

Leanne and I had special respect for bears. Collectively, we'd encountered almost a hundred while hiking, and although nearly every one either fled or was indifferent to our presence, two hadn't. In the latter weeks of our hike from Yellowstone to the Yukon, I had fought off with rocks one that had stalked me and screamed at another that had charged. I had known from the start of this trip that we would see grizzlies—the area was renowned for their abundance—and although I'd done my best to mentally prepare myself, I wasn't ready for them to emerge from their winter dens just yet.

"What would it be eating?" Leanne wondered aloud. I looked at the tracks leading down the same side valley that we would take to the Firth River. Narrow and shaded, the valley was still mostly white.

"Dunno," I said. "Maybe we'll find out."

For the rest of the day, we traveled with the bear tracks under or beside our skis as we wound on and off the ice of Camping Creek, avoiding the intermittent canyons through which water already churned in deep, ice-fringed pools. In 10 miles we saw no hint of bear feeding sites, no places where it had dug for roots or ground squirrels, no berry bushes recently stripped by bear teeth. The ground was frozen, of course, and the berries were months away from emerging. Like us, the bear was hungry and on the move.

"Maybe it'll take us to the caribou," Leanne said.

"Maybe," I answered, unsure whether that was what we wanted. But by the time we'd followed the small tributary to where it spilled into the much wider Firth valley, it was a moot point. The slopes eased back, the shadows disappeared, and we suddenly found ourselves bathed in warm sunlight. I looked south to where the river cut its canyon through the British Mountains, north to where it slows and braids as it passes through the last of the foothills. Except for the higher elevations, I saw no snow. There was no telling where the bear had gone.

"It's a different season here," remarked Leanne as we pulled off our skis and sat down to drink in the springlike scene. Twenty Dall sheep stood a few hundred yards away, their white coats gleaming where they grazed above the river's dark canyon walls, and on the flat, tiered bench that stretched away from them were dozens of ground squirrels, scampering from hole to hole.

"Some of that grass looks like it's already turning green!" I said, but Leanne was looking up, not down, as a ripping sound roared in. Wings flaring at the last possible moment, a diving golden eagle nabbed a ground squirrel, lifting off as others whistled alarm calls that were too late. We watched the bird fly away with its prey dangling beneath it and followed the flapping wings until they became a speck on the northern horizon.

Leanne pointed to something metallic glinting below the disappearing bird.

"The cabin and the shed?"

I nodded and, after sharing the last pinch of the last handful of nuts, got up, tied my skis onto my pack, and led the way.

The padlock was hanging open on the shed when we arrived, and on the snow patch in front of it were fresh bootprints. We pulled open the door and let out a whoop of relief. Not only was all the food we'd asked for present, but the dusty, deflated rubber dinghy was there as well.

"All that's missing are directions for where to find caribou next," I joked. But Leanne was already opening boxes.

"To the park wardens!" she shouted a second later, hoisting a bag of breaded chicken nuggets high in the air.

"To the wardens!" I echoed with a holler, emerging from the shack with a bag of chocolate bars, a tray of donuts, and a fistful of greasy pepperoni sticks.

But the joviality was short-lived. With eyes much bigger than our shrunken stomachs, we consumed far too much in too little time. An hour later, we were splayed out on the tundra with wrappers lying around us, clutching our bloated guts.

"I gotta lie down," Leanne groaned.

I winced. "Me too."

We looked at the river, the cabin beyond it, and back at the river again. Along the Firth, unlike the creek we'd descended earlier that morning, most of the ice shelves were gone, plucked from the canyon walls by rising water levels, which rendered the already swift chasm into a flooding, grinding slurry of churning ice. The thought of mattresses to sleep on, space to spread and dry out our gear, and a floor where we could walk in stocking feet was compelling, but the chasm looked more of a challenge than either of us was willing to face right then. Even if the old rubber raft in the instrument shed was serviceable, we would have to carry it into the canyon, pump it up, load it, and somehow get it across before getting swept into the toilet-bowl-like whirlpool that sucked everything under an ugly-looking ice jam 300 feet downstream.

"It's not going to be straightforward," Leanne admitted.

"Let's tackle it tomorrow," I suggested.

"Tomorrow," she agreed, already unpacking. While she set up the tent, I piled all the food back in the shed.

But sleep didn't come easily. My stomach churned, and we both tossed and turned, giggling like kids as we burped and farted. Before long, I was back outside the tent, squatting, waiting for a purge. But before that could happen, every orifice in my body tightened and the urge to relieve myself suddenly disappeared. A huge, dark grizzly bear had appeared on the canyon rim across the river, and it was looking intently at this strange creature with his pants down around his ankles. I fumbled with my belt buckle, embarrassed and shocked as I hastened back to the tent, but by the time I got there, the bear had stepped back and was gone from view. A few clumps of falling earth and snow were the only signs that the ghostly image had been real.

"Grizzly!" I blurted while unzipping the door.

"Huh?" Leanne had already been asleep.

"A bear," I began, but then realized there was no reason to pull her awake. "It's okay. It took off. I'll tell you in the morning," I said, gently pushing her head back down with a reassuring rub.

When she fell back asleep, I tried to follow after her, but I lay awake a long time instead, listening, trying to remember whether I'd locked the shed door. It didn't matter. The rusty hasp was the weak point. If the bear wanted our food, it would find its way in.

I finally fell asleep but woke with a start a few hours later, screaming as the tent thrashed around us. Something was pushing at the walls, something big, hairy, and powerful.

"Hey! Hey!" I bolted upright in the sleeping bag, already swinging and punching at the tent fabric as I dragged Leanne upright beside me.

"What's going on?" she demanded, blinking at the sight of me with bear spray in one hand and my knife in the other, ready to do battle in my underwear.

Another gust hit and I grew ashamed.

"Uh, nothing," I answered. "I just thought … nothing. It's just the wind."

By the time morning rolled around a few hours later, that wind was another storm, and I was back outside, resecuring guy lines and tie-downs, looking over my shoulder as the fabric bucked and pulled from my hands. There was no cabin to see, no bear, not even a far shoreline in the thickening cloud of wind-whipped snow. Sheets of ice peeled off the water and hurled upstream, shattering against the cliffs below us like panes of glass. I looked to where the cabin had disappeared and couldn't forgive myself for our overindulgence. We were so close—within a few hundred yards—but because of our feasting, we were stormbound in a flapping tent yet again.

> *May 7—Water Survey, Firth River, Yukon*—Survival mode again. We are being baked, frozen, dried, and soaked in an endless endurance test of extremes. It's as if the world doesn't want us to be comfortable, to think there is such a thing as security. I think of the bear hunkered down on the windswept tundra, the ptarmigan huddled in the lee of a leafless bush, the caribou whose sun-warmed slope has turned into a snow-caked maelstrom, and I am embarrassed by my own desires: four solid walls and a good night's sleep.

Two days later, the storm finally eased enough for us to move. Spring had rolled back to winter, and the brown tundra was once again white. Pushing through knee-deep snowdrifts, we dragged our gear and food to the riverbank and, after blowing up the raft and loading it, pushed off.

The river was a little more frozen than when we'd last considered it, but it was still a treacherous mix of unstable ice and fast-flowing water, forcing us to use a combination of ski poles, paddles, and sheer stubbornness to pick, push, and prod our way across. We got hung up in places, and while Leanne leaned precariously out the back, I stepped onto dubious ice shelves out front, pulling with a rope before the footing gave way and I had to dive back onto the pontoons. Finally, after almost a half hour of effort, we reached the other side and, with snow falling again, carried the first of many loads to the cabin sitting above the canyon rim.

"This isn't quite how I remember it," I apologized after the door had swung open. Spreading spots of mildew stained the peeling walls, a couple of rusty bunks with ripped mattresses and missing springs stood against them, and the dishes, table, and floor were covered in a film of mouse droppings and filth. But Leanne didn't seem to mind. Her pack was already off, and she was busy with the broom that had been propped in a corner.

While Leanne cleaned, I wandered outside and did a rough inventory of the junk heap behind the shack. There was a pile of weathered lumber left over from building the cabin, a beat-up old oil heater, some twisted sections of wire, and a collection of rusty barrels and pipe, all of it sifted by the grizzly bear that had spotted me the night before. Noting the paw prints right up to the roofline, I checked the window grates and door hinges, then returned to the junk pile with pocket pliers and our homemade emergency saw. Two hours later, I was standing naked inside the cabin, enjoying the heat as I rinsed off a month's worth of sweat beside a makeshift woodstove.

"How long are we going to stay?" Leanne asked as she finished toweling off with an old dishcloth. It wasn't exactly spotless, but it was a whole lot cleaner than the black water left in the basin where she'd sponge-bathed. Once she was done, she handed the cloth to me, watching as I dried off while I inspected our supplies. There was the original two-week cache of food and fuel, the bit of junk food we hadn't yet consumed, and the box of summer gear we'd requested.

I looked out the window and back at Leanne. It wasn't a full-fledged storm, but it was snowing, and through the cracks around the windows came the whistle of a brisk north wind. What had seemed a good idea three days before—to trade balaclavas for bug shirts, skis for hiking boots, and ski wax for head nets—didn't make much sense now.

"I don't know," I finally admitted. "But we're warm, comfortable, and clean. Can't we just enjoy it?"

Leanne smiled. It wasn't the answer she expected from the

hard-nosed, pushy expedition partner she was accustomed to, but she liked it. I sat down on one of the sagging bunks and she came over, climbing onto my lap for a hug.

"You're getting skinny," I said, wrapping my arms around her bare waist. She gave my beard a tug before running her fingers through my wet hair.

"And you're getting hairy."

I laughed and leaned forward to meet her lips. It wasn't a five-star hotel, but it was as close to a honeymoon as we were going to get.

The contradiction of using modern technology to "be" caribou wasn't lost on either of us, which is why, after another two days of waiting, we debated whether or not to make the call. Our commitment from the beginning was to be guided by what we saw and felt on the ground, not by outside information, but a week of not seeing a single caribou softened that resolve. After much deliberation, I picked up the satellite phone and dialed the Yukon biologist who kept track of the seven radio-collared caribou in the Porcupine Herd.

"Dorothy!" I laughed as her voice came over the phone. "It's Karsten and Leanne."

"Karsten! Where are you?"

"Firth River. About 12 miles inland from the Arctic coast."

"The Firth! Wow! Are you with caribou?" Her voice was hopeful. Having studied the herd for a number of years, Dorothy Cooley was as keen as we were for their amazing story to be told. I tried not to sound too disappointed.

"It's why I'm calling. They spread out about 70 miles ago, back in the Barn Range, and we've seen only a few individuals since."

"Hang on; I'll check the latest locations." While she typed in the website, I listened, catching the sound of other voices chatting and laughing in the background. We'd visited her office the previous winter, and as the sounds came over the line I imagined the warmth, the smell of coffee, the radio playing in the background. It was nothing fancy—an old building tucked at the back of an industrial compound in the gold mining town of Dawson City—but it represented a lot of what we were missing: total comfort, security, and people to talk with beyond ourselves.

"Okay, got 'em," said Dorothy.

I wrote down the coordinates and thanked her, explaining that our call's haste was because we needed to save battery power.

"No problem," she said, signing off. "Good luck and be careful."

For the next hour, Leanne and I sat hunched over the map, plotting locations. Two animals were just north of tree line in Alaska, but it was the five that had wintered in the Yukon that interested us most. We marked their positions, one by one, then leaned back, not quite believing the picture that had emerged. Four were still scattered in the British and Barn mountains behind us, and the lone individual that wasn't was positioned only 20 miles ahead.

"We're near the front!" I exclaimed, double-checking the numbers. "We passed them!" I spun around the cabin, doing a jig.

"What do we do now?" laughed Leanne. I stopped midstride, looked out the window at the shrinking lumber supply, then pointed to the boxes of food beside an old collection of faded books and magazines on a shelf.

"I'm going to cut another load of wood and stoke the fire, and then I'm going to eat, rest, relax, and read."

The shack's library was limited—*Conan the Buccaneer, Conan the Warrior, Conan the Conqueror*, a tattered 1971 issue of *Playboy*, and Alex Haley's *Roots*. We ripped the latter 700-page saga into chapters and began reading it at the same time.

We were most of the way through the thick novel when caribou began arriving late the next day. There were just a few at first, but within an hour there were hundreds perched on the rim of the canyon, peering longingly through the fog toward our side of the river. The Firth was still neither open nor well frozen, and each time a brave individual descended to test the ice, the rest watched from above until an explosion of cracks and pops sent it scurrying back up. A few hundred animals multiplied to more than a thousand, and they spread sideways, searching for a suitable site to cross.

For three days we watched as caribou paced upriver and downriver, unable to fulfill their desire to move on. A few new players wove in and out of the scene—a short-eared owl, a family of foxes, even a wolverine—but they soon departed, leaving us and our hoofed companions on opposite shores, both waiting for conditions to change. Leanne and I needed warm weather so we could walk snow-free to the calving grounds, the caribou needed cold so they could cross a frozen river—but what we got was something in between. The wind died, the fog thickened, and in the diffuse light that followed, the temperature hung at a point that melted only the snow that was falling. Caught between seasons, Leanne and I slept, ate, and watched, losing all sense of day and night.

The grizzly bear reappeared when it got cold again, arriving just before the caribou began to move. But with me napping and Leanne reading, we wouldn't have known it was there had the bruin not come to the cabin and knocked.

"What's that?" I exclaimed, jolting awake as a low thump sounded somewhere in the back corner of the building. Leanne looked up from her book and gave a nonchalant shrug.

"Another ground squirrel?" A whole family of the rodents had been trying to chew up through the floor since we'd arrived.

I shook my head. "Too big." Pulling off the sleeping bag, I walked to where the sound had come from—a hole covered with an old cast-iron pan—and had a look. No sooner had I moved the heavy griddle aside than two ivory claws as long as my middle fingers poked through. I lurched back, a wave of heat prickling across my skin.

"What the...?"

"B-E-A-R," I mouthed. Leanne went wide-eyed, jumping to her feet and sending her book to the floor. But when nothing more than a rubbing sound came in the next few seconds, our fear softened. Tiptoeing to the window, we looked out and confirmed what we already suspected: head back and eyes half closed, the bear was having a good scratch, not trying to break in.

Regardless of the bear's motivations, I was still thankful for the heavy metal grating that covered the windows, for without it, all that would have separated us from an animal four times our weight would have been a ¼-inch-thick pane of glass. And judging from the way it lay down and played with an old wooden ladder, there would have been damage regardless of its good mood. The 80-pound ladder spun in its paws like a pair of chopsticks as the bear twisted and turned it, trying to fit the rungs over its wide head.

"It's huge," Leanne whispered.

I nodded, too absorbed to answer. The bear was in heaven, mouth agape, black nose twitching, its dark eyes rolling in whorls of fur tinged silver and white. It was so beautiful, so close, so playful, nothing like the menacing bruins that I'd been so worried about just a few days before.

Tiring of the game, the bear rolled onto all fours and lumbered out of sight, leaving Leanne and me listening for its next move: the sound of more rubbing, and then a bump that shuddered up one of the windowless walls, sending a quiver through the cabin—and us. It was still playing, we assured ourselves, as the whisking sound of hair on corrugated metal resumed, but when the bumping and jostling migrated toward the door, I instinctively grabbed the handle and held tight with both hands.

The bear never got there; before it rounded the last corner, it encountered the spot where Leanne and I had been urinating for the last eight days, and everything went silent. A grunt finally broke the stillness, followed by two sharp huffs, and then the drum of fleeing paws. I cracked the door, had a good peek, then flung it wide open.

"I've never been inside a bear's rubbing tree before," Leanne said as the dark rump disappeared across the white tundra.

"Me neither," I choked, unsure whether I was shocked, thrilled, or just relieved.

A half hour later the first group of caribou crossed the river, a trickle of animals that, after two days of cold temperatures, found solid ice where none had existed before. Their success sent a silent signal through the valley, and within minutes the miles-long, stagnant front of animals was probing the river in multiple places. Like a dam springing a series of leaks, the previously impassable canyon was breached many times over, draining the reservoir of animals from the opposite bank.

"I guess this means we're skiing to Alaska," I said to Leanne as the first of many groups crested the near side of the canyon and charged past. I watched as they jogged across the bench behind us, then climbed what had become a very white slope. Farther upstream, a triangle of peaks poked through the clouds, looking snowier than any we'd seen so far.

"Guess so." Her voice mirrored the mix of excitement and dread circulating in my own heart. After three weeks without the caribou, being back among the animals was wonderful, but with summer gear to carry on top of everything else, I wasn't looking forward to trying to keep up.

Small, straggling groups were all that remained by the time we were packed and on our way, and they weren't enough to keep our minds off aching shoulders and legs. After a ten-day respite, our muscles revolted at the sudden grind uphill, shocked by the heaviest packs yet. But all the pain and discomfort evaporated when we crested the first ridge: sniffing the same caribou trail we were following was the first of four grizzlies we would see that day.

I don't know whether our reaction was due to the playfulness of the bear the afternoon before or the fact that it had fled soon after realizing we were in the cabin, but Leanne and I were uncharacteristically calm as we pulled out the camera gear and began filming. There were no trees to climb, we carried no gun—all we had for defense was pepper spray and firecrackerlike bear bangers—and yet we watched without any of our usual fear. When a second bruin appeared on the scene a few minutes later, we simply swung the video camera lens toward it and continued to record.

Sight lines were long in the rolling white landscape, and over the next hour we watched as the two bears angled away from each other and us. One took a half-hearted charge at a passing cluster of caribou and the other dug into a snowdrift, but what they mostly were doing was what we'd done before we'd stopped: plodding west on the trails of migrating caribou. The only difference was, they were hoping to find a mishap and a good posthibernation meal.

"Think they're headed to the calving grounds?" I wondered.

"Hope not," said Leanne, "because if they are, they'll soon figure out we're the slowest caribou going." I laughed when she said it, not knowing how accurately it foretold what was to come.

It happened late in the afternoon, just as we were stamping down a patch of snow for the tent. A dark brown bear, larger and woollier than the others, appeared on the horizon and jogged straight into the tight valley where we were planning to camp.

"Hello bear! Here bear!" I said.

It stopped at the sound of my voice, waving its head as it tried to figure out where and what we were. I kept talking as it searched, and it pushed onto its haunches at my gently uttered words.

"Down here, we're down here," I continued in a soft voice, but speaking didn't have the desired effect. Curious, it started toward us again.

"We're here," I said loudly. Waving my arms, I finally shouted. *"Here!"*

It was enough. The bear's eyes finally locked on where we were, and it wheeled around in the same moment, rippling up the slope faster than it had come.

"That was a little too close for comfort," said Leanne as we watched it clamber up the snow and disappear. "Should we still camp here?"

I hesitated.

"Ah, Karst."

"Hang on, I'm thinking."

"Karst." Her tone was insistent.

I turned and saw why. Yet another bear was approaching, contouring across the opposite slope only 200 yards above us—smaller and darker than the one that had just vanished, but a grizzly nonetheless.

"Wow, they're everywhere," I said, hastily gathering my things. Three minutes later, we were packed and slipping through the shadows below the bear—leaving it, the caribou trails, and any other scavengers that might be patrolling the well-worn trenches—in our final bid to escape. One and a half hours and 4 miles later, we found a high bench on a rocky slope and figured we'd gone far enough.

We had set up camp so many times by now that the tasks were automatic. Leanne grabbed the tent, I grabbed the poles, and then we worked together, feeding them into the appropriate sleeves. But midway through the routine, everything stalled. Leanne stopped moving, I turned to see what the matter was, and the bear we thought we'd avoided prowled in.

It was a small, sickly animal, a desperado, and with a chill I realized we were being stalked. Nose on our ski trail and eyes fixed forward, this bear had none of the tentativeness or hesitation that usually accompanies curiosity. After a 4-mile-long hunt, it had made its decision and was closing in for the kill.

To be approached by any wild animal is unnerving; to be approached by a grizzly bear is even more unsettling; but to be approached by a starving grizzly is pure terror. With each successive step it took toward us, I saw more reasons for the bear's brazen behavior: pus-filled eyes, broken claws, a dull coat hanging off a rack of protruding hips, shoulders, and ribs. Playing dead was no option; if it didn't stop soon, we would have to fight back.

When it came within 40 feet I exploded, shouting a string of curses and threats in a spitting, screaming rage. Pulling the bear bangers out of my pocket, I sent the first of two cracker shells skyward, but the one-two booms did nothing to slow the animal's advance. It was deaf as well as desperate. Still, I screamed.

"Get out of here," I screeched, swinging my arms. But still it came, indifferent to my frantic jumps and waves. Grappling for my knife and bear spray, I shouted for Leanne to do the same.

I'd had my share of dreams about marauding bears, but never in the detail that now walked 20 feet away. This was beyond nightmares, beyond imagination, a kind of surreal and fearsome beauty that left us transfixed.

"Oh my God," said Leanne as the bear's lips smacked open and it began to pant. "This is it."

But instead of coming the final few steps, the grinning bear veered at the last moment, bending into a circle that curved not only its trajectory but time as well. Seconds stretched into a prolonged moment, and within that time a sharp vitality took hold, giving me the courage to brandish one of the ski poles and lunge.

My sudden swipes at the air stalled the bruin only for a moment, and when it resumed its advance, I scuttled backward, trading the pole for the tent. It was flimsy and only half set up, but, held high and broadside, it gave the appearance of something large and alien. This time when I lunged, the bear flinched and stepped back.

"Go!" I shouted, pushing forward.

"Go!" echoed Leanne from behind me. It didn't flee but it did retreat, walking, not running, until it disappeared behind a rocky knoll. Still holding the tent, Leanne and I backed into a nearby slope, tripping and falling over the drifts as we tried to see where the bear had gone. Hummocks, hollows, and boulders big enough to hide a bear were everywhere, and after a few fruitless minutes of searching, Leanne kept a lookout while I packed once again.

It was midnight when we reached the ridge top, and with the sun still hanging low on the northern horizon, we searched the triangles of pink light and pools of dark shadow, waiting for something to move. It was a commanding view, and while Leanne silently set up camp, I continued scouring the hillsides, training my binoculars on every dark rock.

"Anything?" she asked when at last I came and sat in the tent doorway.

I shook my head. "Just a string of caribou to the north," I explained, adding how I thought I'd seen the white slate of the Arctic Ocean behind them. "And the peaks of the Brooks Range to the west," I smiled. "Alaska, Leanne! We're getting close."

Her face brightened for a moment, followed by a flush of despair. No matter how upbeat I tried to be, the thought of continuing was too much.

"Karst," she suddenly sobbed, "this is crazy. We're following the caribou to the calving grounds with a bunch of hungry grizzly bears!"

I lay down next to her, feeling a wave of emotion shudder up my spine. It was crazy, I admitted, thinking aloud about what we could do next.

"We could call in a helicopter," I began, almost choking on the words. "We could quit."

Leanne nodded, wiping her tears as I continued.

"Or we could head back to the Water Survey cabin, wait for things to die down, then follow a week or two behind the herd."

"What for?" Leanne asked. "We'd miss them calving."

"Or we could find a place to land a plane—the coast maybe—get picked up, wait somewhere comfortable—Inuvik or the nearest town in Alaska—then get dropped wherever the herd is in a few weeks. By then the ground will be thawed. Plants will be growing. There'll be calves around. Lots of things for bears to eat."

Leanne was silent, waiting for me to utter the final option—which, given how we were feeling right then, didn't seem like much of an option at all.

"Or we could just keep going," I said, "and hope this was just a weird, abnormal day."

I waited for her reaction, but none came. After a few seconds I leaned over, only to find she'd fallen asleep.

> *May 16—Loney Creek, Yukon—*There is no sleep for me. I am too wired, too edgy, too determined to keep watch all night. But what if the bear does come? And if it doesn't, will anything have changed? We have been hunted once, and so long as we stay in this landscape, there is always the possibility of being hunted again.

The old bear didn't come that night, nor did any others. By morning, even the string of caribou had disappeared.

"Nothing in sight," I reported as Leanne sat over the stove melting snow. She hadn't said a thing since awakening a half hour earlier, and I tried to reopen the night's unfinished conversation.

"That really is the Arctic Ocean," I said, trying once more. Looking through binoculars, I described the scene: frozen-in icebergs poking skyward from a sheet of white that glistened and curved over the horizon, stretching as far as I could see.

"And that really is Alaska," I continued, pointing to the western horizon that looked whiter and more jagged than when I'd considered it in the soft light the night before. But Leanne didn't take the bait. It wasn't until we'd finished breakfast that I got a hint of what we were doing next.

"Where are we going?" I asked as she started packing.

"What do you mean, where?" she snapped. She'd slept most of the night, but she looked as haggard as I felt.

"Back? Forward? East? West? Are we keeping on or giving up?"

Leanne gave an impatient sigh. "Wherever the caribou take us."

"Oh," I said, neither happy nor disappointed. "I thought ..."

But the look Leanne gave me said to drop it, and I did.

We encountered two bears over the next 20 miles, and their reactions—bolting at the mere sight of us—were just what we needed for the resolve to continue forward. We moved a little more cautiously now—skiing closer together, shouting out as we approached blind corners, sleeping with bear spray, knives, and a pile of good throwing rocks handy—but it was moving itself that soothed our overactive nerves. As we wound out of the mountains and into the lower foothills, there was a rhythm to our skiing, and as our legs found the old beat, our minds quieted with the familiar, swinging pace.

But just when our anxiety seemed to be fading, another dark shape popped into a scene so similar to the last one that it was strange. We were pitching camp again, in the midst of inserting the second pole into the half-set-up tent, and for a moment I wondered whether we hadn't entered some hidden realm where time circles back on itself, repeating those parts of history we most want to leave behind. But then I realized this was going to be different, very different, for behind the first animal came another two, waltzing over a low ridge 400 yards away.

"I can't believe this," I said, already trembling as I scurried to amass our paltry weapons. But by the time I had the tent pegs pulled and bear bangers, knife, and ski pole in hand, I realized I'd made a mistake. Three bears had multiplied to thirteen.

"Musk ox!" Leanne exclaimed, looking through her binoculars. A flush of embarrassment swept through me, along with relief. Some biologist I was. Size and color are about the only things the prehistoric-looking animals have in common with bears. Hooves, not paws, carry them across the rocky terrain, and long, drooping horns protrude off either side of large, blocky heads. But it is their coats, more than anything, that differentiates them from other animals. They are nearly all hair, dark eyes peering out from woolly mops, and they were traversing the slope above us like a herd of shaggy, oversize mushrooms on legs.

"Quick! Lift the tent!" said Leanne as the docile animals filed past above us. "I think they're coming in!"

I made a mock charge at the still-distant shapes, poking fun at my paranoia. One by one the animals skirted the basin, pausing only long enough to dig through the snow and clip off a rare clump of grass growing among the rocks.

No markers, no flags, and no guards greeted us at the Alaska-Yukon boundary a day later—just a line of caribou tracking across the border without altering their step. It was cold and misty, but we stopped to film anyway, reminding an imaginary audience about the importance of this invisible line. On one side was a nation committed to protecting its share of the calving grounds; on the other was a country pushing to develop its. We were stepping from Canada's Ivvavik National Park, explained Leanne for the camera, into Alaska's Arctic National Wildlife Refuge, which, in a strange twist of fate, fails to protect the caribou where they need refuge the most.

The fog had hung over us all day and our mood was heavy at the border; as we set off again, I tried not to think about what was happening in the skyscrapers and government offices in Houston,

Texas, and Washington, D.C.: More taxpayer-funded subsidies for roads and pipelines. More licenses to pollute air and water. More blind eyes turned to the spills poisoning fish, wildlife, and children. I imagined the suit-and-tie oil lobbyists striding from one senator's office to another, quoting their numbers (stock values, gas prices, gross domestic product, barrels of oil) when the real measures of so-called prosperity lie somewhere else (cancer rates, death tolls, numbers of extinctions). Marbled halls versus snowy valleys; gridlocked highways versus grizzly-dotted foothills; wailing sirens versus the click and clatter of caribou in a quickening wind. The politicians were always talking about rights and freedoms, about liberty and justice, and yet all their maneuverings seemed intent on taking all of that away from a hidden corner of their own country.

I watched as another line of tired-looking cows plodded past. In many ways, I could understand why they didn't garner much compassion from the general public and why the plight of their calving grounds fell on so many deaf ears. They were somewhat ungainly in appearance, not at all the cuddly creatures we are conditioned to care about. And yet hidden behind the oversize necks, skinny legs, and elongated heads is a wisdom that defies their simple, bovine looks.

There was no boundary where we crossed into Alaska, but there was a change in the subsequent days: as we moved within a week's travel of the calving grounds, more and more animals converged on our path, immersing us in a great gathering of life. It was slow at first— just a group of a few dozen caribou trickling out of the headwaters of the Clarence River to join the hundreds we had been following across the foothills—but as we crossed a multitude of smaller creeks and valleys, that trickle became a stream that poured off every ridge and hillside.

"Ours was just one path," I muttered to Leanne as honking geese and swans flocked past in loose, V-shaped strings while more caribou streamed in.

"Pardon?"

"One of many journeys," I repeated as chattering white-crowned sparrows, horned larks, and Lapland longspurs flitted through the pussy willows all around us. As I watched them hop from leafless branch to leafless branch, I thought back on the rush of animals we'd followed through the Richardsons and on the wolf chases, the blizzard, and the grizzly bear encounters we'd endured since. What predators had they passed, I wondered, watching them flap off and battle the north wind; what storms, hunger, and exhaustion? Ours was just one thread of one migration, I suddenly realized, one chapter in a multitude of stories that now, after collectively covering millions of miles across the land and through the air, were converging onto Alaska's endangered coastal plain.

> *May 24—Unnamed creek west of Clarence River, Alaska*—To move with such a gathering of life is intoxicating, but as the weather warms and the snow trails melt beneath us, the thrill matures into a deep honor. Hours-old tracks give way to ruts underneath, carved deep into the rocky ground by millions of hooves. It is more than trails we have been following. Each path is a respun strand in an ancient blanket, an intricate stitch work covering four mountain ranges, two countries, and every valley, plain, and peak in a living, breathing, pulsing web.

It was there, immersed in the history and energy of multiple migrations, that I clearly heard what had registered as only a subtle rumbling before. I had felt hints of it during those first days when the caribou had charged past us in the Richardsons, and again when large groups had filed past our camp in the Driftwood valley. But that had been early in the trip, a time when so much was new and overwhelming, and I'd forgotten about it in the excitement and stress of all that had happened since. Now, however, camped in a corner of the Alaskan foothills with thousands of caribou and birds suddenly coursing all around us, it was more than a hint. The land was vibrating underneath me, as though the ground itself were alive.

I had to tell Leanne.

"Listen!" I nudged her sleeping body as I cracked open the tent door. Within yards of where we lay, dozens of animals stood in the fog, jostling for a few sprigs of snow-free grass.

"Leanne!" I whispered, but still she slept, leaving me alone to puzzle whether the thrumming I heard was real. A trained scientist, I was vexed by its formlessness: neither loud nor subtle, it was a strong beckoning I could hardly hear. Propped on one elbow while the caribou shuddered and grunted all around me, I strained to tease out the baseline melody humming through the ground.

I tried one more time: "Leanne! Do you *feel* that?" But still she slept.

I lay back, wondering if I was imagining things, and if not, what the thrumming meant. Was the sound because of the convergence of all the animals, or was the convergence prompted by the sound? Did it come and go, or was it me who was changing, hearing something that had always existed, only noticing it for the first time?

The thrumming was still there when we set off again the next morning—not as loud but still buzzing in the background, a hum that spread across the next two valleys and spilled over the pass between. Leanne didn't hear it, but that didn't seem to matter. Schussing down the other side to the Kongakut River, we were in the flow of animals again, and that was enough. We were part of something larger, a communal push that was closing in on the mysterious place that had kept all of us moving for so long.

I watched the cows we'd been following all day step into the river and wade up to their chests. There was no hesitation anymore, no stopping to feed, rest, or deliberate. As wide as barrels, they seemed to float more than wade across, guarding their bellies as they hauled themselves onto the ice of the opposite shore. And then they took off: not running—they were too pregnant for that now—but rushing nonetheless, not bothering even to shake off the water before resuming their brisk walk.

I wanted nothing more than to keep following them, to stay in the wash of life crossing both upstream and downstream of where we stood, but with just 40 miles left to go to the calving grounds, we had to stop and wait. We were just three days shy of the place we'd heard, read, and imagined so much about—but we'd run out of food again.

Of the thirteen caches we'd packaged in Inuvik, we'd sent three by mail to Walt Audi, who, along with his wife, Merilyn, runs a small hotel, restaurant, and flying business in Kaktovik, a small Inupiat village on Barter Island just offshore of the Arctic National Wildlife Refuge. We'd talked to him twice already, first to make sure the packages had arrived and then again from the Firth River to say we were getting close.

"So you're at the Kongakut and want food?" he said when I reached him this time. "What does it look like out there?"

I described the flat gravel bar free of snow and ice and how we could see old tire tracks where a plane had landed before.

"I know the place," said Walt after I'd described it in more detail. "Now, am I just dropping off boxes there, or am I bringing you guys in for a cleanup and a good feed?"

Leanne pulled back from where she'd been leaning over the earpiece and shot me an excited glance.

"Bring us in?" I repeated.

"Yeah, you know, take a break before continuing," he chuckled. "Or have you two really turned into caribou?"

I hesitated, seduced by images of warm showers, a comfortable bed, and an unlimited supply of food. Leanne practically jumped beside me. "I'll get back to you."

"No problem," said Walt. "There's another fog bank coming anyway. The soonest I can come is tomorrow afternoon."

The fog bank did come, and it was within its damp grasp that Leanne and I deliberated in the tent while caribou continued to pass outside. It was a passionate discussion, the closest thing to a fight we'd had yet, Leanne pushing for us to take Walt's offer and me arguing to turn it down.

"C'mon, Karst. Three or four days. What's the harm in that?"

But I was adamant. The seasons were about to change, we were almost at the calving grounds, and much of the mental clutter—the crummy songs and old phone numbers, forgotten birthdays and other useless facts that had surfaced earlier—was gone. I thought back on the old stalking bear, the storm at the Blow River, the fifty days of skiing— and then I thought of the thrumming. It was all connected: the scares had unseated old patterns of naming, studying, and understanding; the miles had led to new ways of knowing and hearing. But it had taken miles and weeks for it to happen.

Leanne rolled her eyes. "Don't be such a purist. Just think: we could meet some of the Inupiat people and find out why they support oil drilling." She poked me in the ribs. "We could put on some weight. Besides," she pointed out the tent door, "the caribou seem more wary. Maybe it's not so bad if we stay away for a few days."

She had a point. The caribou were more skittish. Even groups crossing the river 300 yards away from us looked repeatedly at our tent. A week before, they would have passed within a few dozen yards and not given it a second glance. But despite all Leanne's arguments, going in still didn't feel right.

"I don't know," I said, ducking out the door when there was a lull in the procession of caribou that continued to pass. "I'm going for a walk."

Minutes later, I was back.

"A bear," I stammered, trying to hide the old panic as it took hold again. "Heading this way!"

Leanne looked out, but the fog had obscured the bear and its approach. Heart pounding and armpits sweating, I forgot every wilderness ideal I'd talked about as I reached for the phone.

"Hello, Walt? Yeah, it's Karsten. Get in here quick as you can."

kaktovik

There's a lightness in things. Only we people move forever burdened,
pressing ourselves onto everything, obsessed by weight.
How strange and devouring our ways must seem
to those for whom life is enough.
    —Rainer Maria Rilke, *Sonnets to Orpheus*, Part Two, XIV

"T his is it," said Merilyn as we bumped through the last few potholes
and rolled to a stop. I peered through the cracked windshield of
the aged pickup at the piles of old fuel drums and derelict machinery.

"Where's Kaktovik?"

"This *is* Kaktovik," she assured us. Leanne and I looked at each
other, wondering if it was a joke. Walt, who hadn't said much since
picking us up on the Kongakut, stayed quiet as he opened the door.

"And the hotel?"

"Right there!" said Merilyn, exasperated. She pointed as Walt
hopped across a couple of mud puddles and plodded across a trail
of wooden pallets to two decrepit trailers tacked together with faded
scraps of plywood and sheet metal. "Welcome to Waldo Arms Hotel,"
proclaimed a tired old sign tacked beside the door.

The inside of Waldo's was a bit more encouraging. In among the industrial tools, cardboard boxes, and other junk piled in the corners were a couple of comfortable couches and a kitchen whose grill and deep fryer promised a good, greasy feed. While Merilyn readied our room, Leanne and I perused the outdated calendars, faded posters, and framed photographs that decorated the dining room walls. The photographs, taken by professional wildlife photographers who had stayed at Waldo's, were impressive: herds of caribou dashing through rivers under the midnight sun, foxes asleep at the mouth of their den, bloody-faced polar bears gnawing at the washed-up carcasses of whales. But it was the poster of radio-collared caribou locations, meant to be updated every two weeks, that intrigued me the most. I went over hoping to compare the locations of the marked animals in the Porcupine Herd with our own movements. No such luck. The last time anybody had bothered to update the poster was four years earlier, in September 1999.

"Your room is ready," Merilyn chirped down the hallway. Leanne and I traced the sound of her voice to a musty cubbyhole, where she was fussing with the torn polyester cover on one of the twin beds. The door on the fiberboard closet hung by a single hinge, and the wood panel walls bore the punch and kick marks of someone who'd probably stayed a little too long because of bad weather.

"How much a night?" I asked.

Merilyn stalled. "It's got satellite TV," she said, fingering the remote control. "Hundreds of channels."

"How much?"

Merilyn looked at the floor. "One hundred fifty dollars per person per night."

"What?" I coughed. "Three hundred for the two of us? What about other hotels?"

"There's only one, and it's closed."

I hesitated while Leanne shifted uncomfortably beside me.

"And I wouldn't camp if I were you," added Merilyn, reading my mind. "There's a polar bear prowling around town. Fresh tracks on the airstrip this morning. Last night it came up to someone's house."

Our reaction to the hotel rates had reached Walt by the time we made our way back to the kitchen, and he offered to cut us a generous deal. I thanked him, trying not to salivate as he hoisted a gallon jug of cooking oil over the grill.

"Well, are you just going to stand there and drool, or are you going to get cleaned up?" he joked, slapping down a row of frozen beef patties in anticipation of the evening rush.

The dirt and dried sweat came off in sheets, and it took three shampoos before I even got a lather, but when I emerged from the shower, my whole body tingled with the unique sensation of being clean. I rubbed at the steamed mirror and saw a stranger stare back at me with bloodshot eyes, a thickening beard, and a red, weather-beaten face. I combed my thinning hair with a few fingers, rubbed the dried skin peeling from my nose, and examined a few bumps on my forehead that threatened to mature into pimples. It had been months since I'd even thought about my appearance, much less worried about it, but one glance in a mirror changed everything. I emerged from the bathroom more self-conscious than when I'd gone in.

"You look ... funny," said Leanne, rubbing my fluffy hair and inadvertently starting a shower of dandruff in the process. I returned the gesture, telling her she looked beautiful as I patted her newly voluminous curls.

A mob of hungry Inupiat customers had arrived while we'd showered, and I nodded hello to every one of them as I inched my way to the kitchen window. But Walt didn't play favorites, no matter how hungry they were. What ensued was a torturous two-hour wait.

"So where'd you come from?" asked one of the teenagers as she bit into her Waldo burger.

"From Old Crow," answered Leanne, doing her best not to stare hungrily. "In the Yukon. We've been following the caribou on skis." But either the girl and her friends didn't believe us, or they weren't interested, for they responded with a few giggles and nonchalant shrugs, then casually turned the conversation back to small talk, telling us who in town had the newest snowmobile and what had happened in the latest episodes of their favorite series on TV. Leanne and I smiled and nodded politely for a few minutes, then excused ourselves and retreated to our room.

When Walt finally called, we had to keep ourselves from running. It was late—9:00 PM—and the ranks of customers had thinned enough that there could be no mistaking for whom the last two burgers and plates of fries had been made. Trying hard not to embarrass ourselves, Leanne and I ate as slowly as possible. Judging by Walt's and Merilyn's reactions, though, it wasn't very slow at all.

"You'd think they were starving," said Merilyn.

"Think?" I exclaimed between mouthfuls. "We are!" Taking the hint, Walt clambered back to the kitchen, reemerging with a couple of pieces of leftover chicken, two thick wedges of chocolate sponge cake, and a bowl of ice cream each.

"So what's new in the world?" I asked after I'd stuffed in the last spoonful and pushed back the pile of plates. Walt looked at Merilyn as he fingered his gray ponytail, then glanced across at Leanne and me.

"Not much except the war with Iraq." He spat out the words, watching me for a reaction. "Oh, I forgot," he added after a few seconds. "You guys are Canadian. There's a SARS epidemic somewhere in Ontario, and a case of mad cow disease has the beef ranchers in Alberta worried."

Leanne frowned beside me. Neither of us had thought about world news in a long time, and it seemed a strange and fruitless subject for two people whose only concern had been to follow caribou each day. There was an immediacy in the way we'd lived over the last seven weeks, and news of bigger problems elsewhere—things we couldn't do anything about—hit with an unwanted weight. Excusing ourselves from the conversation, we waddled back to our room, closed the curtains, and climbed into our separate beds.

I awoke disoriented, grasping for reasons why Leanne wasn't beside me in the sleeping bag and why the twenty-four-hour daylight had suddenly gone dark. But then the smell of soap and the scratch of nylon brought me into the present, and I reached onto the bedside table for my watch. Thirteen hours had passed. It was time to eat again.

Breakfast ran into lunch, lunch into midafternoon nap time, and nap time was followed by a predinner snack. Between it all, a few new hotel guests and restaurant customers floated in: workers for the military's nearby Distant Early Warning radar station, glaciologists taking ice cores from the nearby mountains, an old Inupiat woman who remembered times when she ate nothing but seals and caribou, and a steady stream of soda pop–seeking kids.

But it was Roger Kaye, a Fairbanks-based U.S. Fish and Wildlife Service pilot, who made the biggest impression, because it turned out he was the Arctic National Wildlife Refuge's chief historian as well. The bespectacled fifty-something man who was staying in town overnight had barely finished dinner before he started to quote speeches and letters from early conservation stalwarts such as Aldo Leopold, Bob Marshall, George Collins, Thomas Berger, and Olaus and Margaret Murie who had pushed hard in the 1950s and '60s to get the refuge protected. Having heard it all before, Walt and Merilyn drifted from the table, but Leanne and I stayed, listening as Roger continued, unfazed.

"Back in the fifties, the issue was more about values than ecology," he told us. "Prosperity and growth were unprecedented in America, and a few people stepped back to ask an important question: will human intention leave any patch of soil untouched?"

"Still relevant today," Leanne cut in.

Roger smiled. "Caribou factored into the campaign in those early years, but only as a symbol. The issue wasn't about the survival of caribou but the survival of what they represented: freedom, wildness, and the ability to roam wherever they pleased."

Leanne and I nodded, knowing exactly what he meant.

"And it worked," he beamed. "In 1960, Secretary of the Interior Fred Seaton protected the area under executive proclamation. In 1980 President Carter doubled its size."

"Except for the 1002 lands on the coastal plain," interjected Leanne.

"Except for the 1002 lands," agreed Roger. The biological heart of the refuge, the 1002 lands provide calving caribou with vital food in a unique haven.

"And so the fight continues," Roger slapped the table. "But today it's different. We're studying why and when and where animals move instead of celebrating the mystery. We're forgetting about the freedom! Science has its strengths," he continued more quietly, "but it also has problems. Our computer models imply we understand what's too complex to know, and yet we spend huge amounts of time and money trying to nail down what can't be quantified or defined."

"Like whether or not oil and caribou mix," I interrupted.

Roger nodded. "Exactly."

"So what would happen if oil and gas development did proceed on the coastal plain?" I asked.

"If?" Roger asked. "It already has! Just look at Prudhoe Bay and the National Petroleum Reserve," he said, pointing west. "Ninety-five percent of Alaska's Arctic coast is already open or is in the process of being opened to oil and gas development. The Arctic National Wildlife Refuge is only 5 percent of it, and it's all that's left!" Roger paused, then remembered the question. "What would happen?" He shook his head. "In terms of caribou and birds and wolves and bears, I'm not sure. Nobody is. But there would be no question the intent of the refuge would be violated. It was meant to be the ultimate symbol of human restraint. To be left untouched. Something sacred would be desecrated …" Roger grasped at the air to better express himself. "It would be like building a video arcade in the Sistine Chapel," he declared. "In a world filled with compromise, the refuge is one of the few sacrosanct things we have left."

The storm that had swept in soon after we'd landed in Kaktovik eased that night, giving way to a warm front that flooded the coast the next day. After another big Waldo breakfast, we stepped into sunshine and stillness that had the mercury sitting at a balmy 10 degrees Fahrenheit above freezing. Suddenly it was summer by Kaktovik standards, and the kids were out in droves, chucking snowballs in shorts, tee shirts, and sandals, while a couple of adults wrestled a whining portable pump into the growing puddles around town. A handful of trucks, four-wheelers, and bicycles zipped back and forth on the grid of eight gravel streets, and behind the bustle the DEW-line station hummed, churning out a steady supply of microwaves.

On the recommendation of Walt and Merilyn, we went to visit Isaac Akootchook, an Inupiat elder who doubled as the local Presbyterian preacher—a squat, moon-faced man whose lined eyes and cheeks suggested he'd spent a good portion of his eighty years laughing. But when he saw Leanne's video camera, a look of seriousness replaced the gaiety, and he launched into a well-rehearsed statement about oil and gas development in the Arctic National Wildlife Refuge and where his people stood. Hundreds of television and film crews had been there before us, and nothing we said could dissuade him from thinking we weren't just another pair of nameless interviewers out to create another piece of polarized news. And so we got the same lines he'd fed everyone else: the Inupiat welcome the promise of jobs and revenue and are strong enough as a people and community to ensure that anything that proceeds will be done in a way that doesn't threaten the plants, animals, and water they rely on for subsistence. He was short on specifics and, after ten minutes of rambling, ushered us out the door.

Unconvinced, we headed for Kaktovik's municipal office and fell into conversation with the mayor. Lon Sonsalla was younger than Isaac, in his forties, and as an import from Wisconsin, he spoke about the issue with more caution. But the gist of his argument was the same: living in Kaktovik is harsh and expensive, and if it isn't oil and gas revenues, then what is it going to be? "People aren't going to go back to living in igloos and tents," he said. "Technology is good now. There's directional drilling. This could be done without harming the environment or the caribou. The people of Kaktovik will make sure."

I held my tongue, reminding myself we were soliciting an opinion, not entering into an argument, but it was obvious the mayor hadn't read the cover story of the *Anchorage Daily News* the day before. Another pipeline in the nearby Prudhoe Bay oil field had ruptured, spilling 2,000 gallons of crude oil, gas, and contaminated water on the tundra just as migratory birds were arriving to nest. Another 1,700-gallon accident had happened earlier in the week and, according to a report from the state of Alaska's own Department of Environmental Conservation, those were just two of an average of 504 spills that contaminated Alaska's North Slope with tens of thousands of gallons of crude oil each year. Leanne and I thanked Lon for his time and walked back into the sunshine, wondering how the oil companies had earned his faith.

In dire need of inspiration, Leanne and I went for a walk. A cheery chorus of snow buntings sang from the powerlines, but they weren't cheery enough. Sauntering down the only road that left town, we soon found ourselves passing the droning generator station, the sewage and garbage dumps, and bits of plastic, Styrofoam, and iridescent slicks of oil that had rafted together on every tundra pond. We scaled the gravel pile where the road ended and climbed down to a line of whale ribs jutting from the ice on the beach. The huge bones were all that remained of a bowhead that the Inupiat had harvested and butchered two years earlier, but the pungent smell of decaying flesh still hung in the air. A mix of old and new polar bear tracks approached from all directions, and tufts of silver and white hair on the biggest rib fluttered in the breeze. I thought about the stunning photographs of white bears with red faces on the wall in Waldo's; the multimillion-dollar polar bear–watching industry in Churchill, Manitoba, in northern Canada; and Lon's open-ended question: *if not oil and gas, then what's it going to be?* The answer seemed obvious.

Robert Thompson was someone who knew about photographers and polar bears. We met the owner of Kaktovik Arctic Adventures the next day and, after introducing ourselves, sat down for a chat in his living room. Pamphlets from the Sierra Club, the Wilderness Society, and the Center for Biological Diversity sat beside musk-oxen horns on side tables, and on the floor lay a thick binder with the latest environmental impact statement for more oil development near the already bustling Prudhoe Bay. When Robert wasn't out guiding people to see wild animals, he was keeping himself informed of the threats to wildlife.

"About 75 percent of the people around here are in favor of oil and gas development on the 1002 lands," said Robert matter-of-factly, "but few of them truly know what it would mean. It's too bad, because you don't have to go very far to see what would happen. It's all visible right in Nuiqsut."

"Nuiqsut?" I asked.

"Yeah, a small Inupiat village along the coast near the Prudhoe Bay oil complex. About 180 miles west of here. You've probably heard their mayor talking about it. She's very outspoken about the problems."

Leanne and I shook our heads.

"Oh, well, let me fill you in," said Robert. "There were lots of promises about employment and money when Prudhoe was being developed in the late sixties, and some of them were fulfilled. But some serious problems came with the benefits. Alcoholism skyrocketed, as did respiratory problems in children, and there was a sharp rise in child abuse and suicide. Not to mention the hunting," Robert chuckled. "One guy got arrested when a stray bullet hit a pipeline. Now, people have trouble finding caribou at all." Robert stared at the floor for a few seconds, then sighed. "The place is broken and nobody knows how to fix it. Meanwhile, the oil wells are drying up and the companies are looking for other places to go."

We all sat in silence for a moment, watching motes of dust swirl in the shafts of sunlight streaming through the windows.

"So why are people so keen for it to come here?" Leanne asked.

Robert smiled and rubbed a thumb and finger together. "The usual reason. The Inupiat of Kaktovik own approximately 96,000 acres in the 1002 lands. I'm not sure I believe it, but I've heard it said the sale of mineral rights to those private lands would mean every one of Kaktovik's 300 residents would become millionaires."

"What about you?" Leanne pressed. "You're Inupiat, aren't you?"

"I'm Inupiat but not from this village. It's my wife's family that lives here. They would benefit from the deal, but not me," he confessed. "Me, I don't want development. I don't want it because of what it would do to the community, as well as the birds, wildlife, and land."

> *May 30—Kaktovik, Alaska*—I don't know who or what to believe anymore. Nothing is as straightforward or openly honest as it was with the caribou. Overnight millionaires importing more plastic, more engines, more fuel—more things to promote the uncoupling

of humans from their natural surroundings—while the piles of garbage and contaminated soil continue to build. There is nothing real about an economic system that measures prosperity in dollars and material goods when the real wealth—clean air, pure water, abundant wildlife, and the freedom to move— is further compromised with each dollar made.

Kaktovik was to have been a break from the drudgery of following the caribou, but after four days in town, we realized it was that very drudgery and the simplicity that came with it that we yearned for. True, we were cleaner and better fed than when we'd arrived—we'd each gained 7 pounds, thanks to Walt's high-fat cooking—but the overall experience left us feeling tainted and empty. We agreed that if we could do it all over again—if we could turn back the clock and plant ourselves back on the Kongakut River the week before—our decision would have been different.

Walt was gruff at the best of times, so I prepared myself before approaching him about flying us back to be with caribou, but I still wasn't ready for the curtness of his negative response. The thaw was underway and the rivers were flooding. There was no place he could land and drop us off, he told me. Like it or not, we would just have to wait. Hurrying back to our room, I broke the news to Leanne, then pulled out the map. It would take us five or six days to walk to the preferred calving area around the Jago River, and by then, most of the cows would probably have given birth.

"Maybe someone could get us close by snowmobile," Leanne suggested, but a quick phone call to Robert confirmed what we already suspected: the melting ice between the island and mainland was unsafe, the snow across the coastal plain was too soft, and the open creeks and rivers would be impossible to cross. The irony was too painful to swallow. The desire for a few days of comfort was about to rob us of what we'd endured almost two months of hardship to see. The caribou were calving and we were stuck in a prodevelopment town using a credit card we couldn't afford.

Worried and unable to sleep, I got up early the next morning and, as chance would have it, overheard the telephone conversation of a young helicopter pilot who had flown in during the night. He was waiting to pick up a team of glaciologists camped at the head of the Jago River, I heard him explain to his boss, and although there was too much fog at the moment, he would fly as soon as he could. I pounced on him the moment he hung up.

The sun broke through at ten o'clock. An hour later we were airborne, the tanks, shipping containers, satellite dishes, and drifted-in boats of Kaktovik shrinking beneath us in a haphazard puzzle of colors and shapes. It had been a rush getting ready—I ran across town to give our skis away to Robert, while Leanne mailed the rest of our winter gear home from the post office—but we really were on our way, outfitted with a ski pole each for walking, a pair of hiking boots, our usual packs full of equipment, and a two-week supply of food.

The fog had lifted from Kaktovik, but it was still thick over the coastal plain, and within ten minutes of leaving we were flying just a few dozen yards off the ground.

"C'mon, where's the hole? Where's the hole?" chanted the pilot as we zigzagged over the tundra. But there was no hole, just a thickening blanket of mist that squeezed us closer to the ground. Twisting and turning, we wove from light spot to light spot, only to have them darken by the time we arrived. Disoriented and confused, the pilot pulled back on the control stick and punched buttons on the Global Positioning System device.

"Any idea where we are?" he asked, holding us in a hover 100 feet off the ground. I unfolded a map from my pocket and searched for a pattern that fit the wet scene below. From what I could tell, the entire coastal plain was covered in shallow ponds and winding creeks like the ones flooding beneath us now.

"There!" he pointed, swerving the machine toward another bright spot, but it soon closed like all the others, pushing us down until the skids almost touched the ground. Birds flushed from the wet bushes as he carefully eased us forward, inching the ship through the fog.

"Caribou!" Leanne suddenly shouted as a brown streak fled beneath us. Behind it, a dark shape wobbled to its feet, tried to follow, then collapsed. "And a calf!"

"That's it," swore the pilot, veering around. "We're heading back."

"Wait!" I insisted. I glanced back at Leanne and knew from her look that she agreed with what I was about to say. "Drop us here, please."

"What? Here?" The pilot scanned the puzzle of flooding creeks, meltwater pools, and patches of soft snow. "Are you crazy?"

I checked with Leanne again and she nodded in a way that said she'd swim all of it before going back to Kaktovik.

"We'll be fine," I assured him. "Please, just put us down."

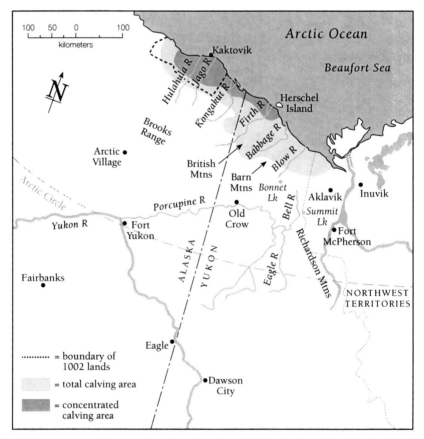

CALVING GROUNDS OF THE PORCUPINE CARIBOU HERD

calving

Life holds mystery for us yet. In a hundred places
we can still sense the source: a play of pure powers
that—when you feel it—brings you to your knees.
　　　　　　—Rainer Maria Rilke, *Sonnets to Orpheus*, Part Two, X

L eanne bumped me for the umpteenth time as she shifted positions.

"Are they still out there?" she asked.

I unfolded my knees and ankles as I carefully squeezed past the mound of gear she'd pushed aside in order to cook, then I leaned out the door. Thirty yards away lay eight cows waiting to give birth, while behind them stood two others, each nursing a wobbly-legged calf.

"How many?" Leanne whispered after I'd nodded.

I squinted into the fog, trying to make out shadows and ghostlike shapes. Hundreds. Maybe thousands. For all I knew, every pregnant cow in the 123,000-member herd was out there. Until the weather cleared, it was impossible to say.

We hadn't gone far after the pilot had dropped us off—500 yards, perhaps—before half a dozen cows had flushed out of the bushes and waddled off looking very pregnant and very agitated. Feeling terrible, we'd pitched camp right there despite the standing water, assuming the soggy campsite would suffice for a few hours until the animals drifted on. But then six cows became twelve, and the following hours brought dozens more. They'd lain down around us. They'd waited. And although more had arrived, none had moved off.

We had tried to go outside, but each attempt had set off a wave of panic among the cows. They were now, unlike in the spring migration, suddenly intolerant of our presence, skittish and paranoid, bolting from as far as a quarter mile away. It took a few tries before we realized what was happening. We couldn't continue walking; we couldn't even stretch. Those animals that had given birth were protective of their newborns, and those that hadn't were so vigilant and sensitive that we couldn't so much as stand upright and take a step. Surrounded by calving caribou, we had become hostages in our tent.

It was a position most wildlife photographers would die for, and yet we were miserable. After five days of sitting in Kaktovik, it was movement we craved, not more rest, a yearning that spun in our heads as much as itched in our feet. In less than a week, we'd been yanked from wilderness to industrial society and back again, and our spirits were struggling to adjust to the transitions that the plane and helicopter had rendered so abrupt. We were only 50 miles from where Walt had plucked us from the bank of the Kongakut River six days earlier, and yet everything had changed: the weather, the bird songs that filled the foggy air around us, the amount of snow, and the caribou themselves. Disoriented and unsettled, we wanted to walk again—to feel the rhythms that had helped connect us to the land and the caribou on their spring migration—but our ability to do so had changed as well.

"I'm going out to pee," said Leanne, starting out the back door. I nodded, holding a finger to my lips as she elbowed past, scrunching me against the wall. But she needed no reminding that caribou were right outside. Her knees hadn't even left the tent before she was crawling back inside.

"They're freaking out," she explained.

I gestured toward her cup as she crossed her legs in desperation. We'd both done it during the blizzard—saving the hassle of getting dressed to brave the elements—but those had been special circumstances. Now, Leanne refused—but after a half hour of waiting, she couldn't wait any longer.

"Let me get this straight," she said while hauling down her pants. "The oil companies figure they can build and operate airstrips here. They say they can have pumping stations, pipelines, roads, and drill pads and still not disturb the animals . . . but I can't even step outside this tent?"

I laughed, turning away to give her privacy, trying not to listen as our 4-by-6-foot bedroom—which had now also become our living and eating area—became a bathroom as well.

It wasn't until the next morning that the fog and light rain lifted and, for the first time since stepping out of the helicopter four days before, we saw where we sat. An aqua blue river ran on one side of us, a low grassy bump rose up from the flat expanse of tussocks on the other, and straight ahead, stretching back into the straw-colored foothills of the Brooks Range, was a wide basin dotted with thousands of caribou. I looked up, way up at the jagged white and blue peaks that towered as high as 9,000 feet behind them, and the value of this place hit home. Hemmed in by towering glaciers on one side and a frozen ocean on the other, the 20-mile-wide coastal plain is a precious strip of fertile ground.

"Good morning," I beamed, kissing Leanne hard as she sat up and rubbed her eyes.

"Morning?" She looked at her watch. "It's 3:30 AM."

"An exhilarating, wonderful, caribou-filled morning," I said, leaning toward her again. She deflected my second advance and leaned forward to peer out the door. Within seconds, she understood my sudden shift in mood.

Despite the hour, the sun was already climbing from its night run across the northern horizon, and all that had been drab and gray in the days before now glimmered in the early morning light. The brown grass had turned gold, the eyes of every caribou shone silver, and the buds on every bush hung like diamonds in the fiery, low-angle light. Even the sounds had changed: instead of the caws and screams of ravens and jaegers that had dominated the misty days before, the voices of songbirds now filled the air—Lapland longspurs, white-crowned sparrows, snow buntings, and horned larks—whistling and trilling to attract a mate.

"What's that?" whispered Leanne a few minutes later.

"What's what?" I asked. The place was layered in sound.

"That," said Leanne when something broke through the melodies. It wasn't a song she was referring to but a sputtering cough. Scanning every bush and hollow, we honed in on the hacking wheeze. Not 40 yards away, a cow caribou lay on her side, panting on a patch of snow.

"She's in labor," whispered Leanne.

I nodded, hopeful that because the fog had lifted, we might actually see what transpired. A handful of other cows had reached the same point over previous days, but all had walked into the mist to give birth out of sight. Grabbing our respective cameras, we jostled for the best vantage, threw fingers for who got the tripod, then positioned ourselves at the door.

For the next half hour we watched as the cow rose, took a few steps, then dropped to the ground again, switching from one side to the other in an attempt to get comfortable. There were other cows in the vicinity, but they paid her little attention, continuing to graze and doze as they waited for their own time to come. Finally, after staggering from snow to wet tussocks and back again, the laboring cow found a rare patch of dry tussocks and settled in.

Compared to the hardships and effort the caribou had endured to get here, birth seemed remarkably quick and easy for her. Lying sideways, she looked once over her shoulder, gave a few pushes, then sent the dark, wet bundle into the world with one smooth heave.

"It's tiny," enthused Leanne as the cow rose and turned to lick the shiny, football-size calf clean. Behind the cow, the silvery rope of the broken umbilical cord swung against her blood-stained legs.

"And determined," I whispered as a miniature muzzle rose above the tussocks and suckled at the air in jerky sweeps. It disappeared for a moment, rose again, then climbed even higher as the calf struggled to its feet. Leanne looked up from the viewfinder in disbelief.

"It's already standing!"

Indeed, less than five minutes after being born, the calf had levered itself upright on what appeared to be a very generous helping of legs. It was comical how long they were—four stiltlike limbs wedged under a tiny body, each going its own way as new nerves short-circuited the fledgling muscles sheathed under a layer of short, brown fur and paper-thin skin. Struggling for control, the calf pitched forward and toppled, staying on the ground only as long as it took to gather itself and try again.

It took three attempts to reach the fur of its mother's underbelly, two to find the udder, and one more to latch onto a teat, but when it did, there was no letting go. For the next few minutes Leanne and I watched as the calf's body gyrated with the flow of warm milk into its belly, quietly laughing as waves of pleasure ran the length of its quivering body, from slurping lips to the white, vibrating tail. I looked at my watch as the calf fed. Seventeen minutes had passed since it had been born. In another fifteen, it would take its first steps and a life of journeying would begin.

I don't know whether it was the beauty of the birth, the clearing weather, the remarkable views, or a mixture of all three that made the difference, but our spirits lifted that morning. For the first time in days, we didn't mind the sitting. In fact we relished it, for moving would have meant missing not only the calf's arrival but also the flush of life that came behind it. It was as if a switch had been thrown, releasing all the energy and potential that had gathered for weeks around us, sending it spilling onto the coastal plain. Killdeers, sandpipers, and other shorebirds flew in with brant geese on a wave of wings, while bees, butterflies, and swallows drifted and swooped in and out of view. It was a dance that everything was doing—the mergansers that glided in and plied the braided channels of the nearby river, the ground squirrels that darted in and out of their burrows, the pair of longspurs that, after days of subdued courting, copulated in front of our tent in a sudden flutter of wings. Even the new caribou mothers had fresh energy, running ahead a few steps before stopping to encourage their newborns to follow, grunting and bobbing their approval with each of the calves' shaky steps.

Everything seemed to be celebrating life, to be rejoicing in its beauty, and we threw open the tent doors in an effort to be part of it all, marveling as clusters of arctic poppies and mountain avens erupted in yellow and white blooms. We still couldn't move because of caribou, we were still relegated to sitting, but it was no longer confining. Having been forced to watch, we couldn't help but appreciate what was happening around us. Because of the caribou, we'd stumbled onto the riches of being still.

> *June 5—Jago River, Alaska*—The sheer volume of life
> is overwhelming, but it's the timing of its arrival that
> is most impressive. Not more than a week ago, we
> were skiing across a snowy landscape that contained
> little food for the tens of thousands of exhausted
> caribou cows, and it held no hint of the protein-rich
> grass they would require to produce milk for their
> soon-to-be-born calves. There were no flowers for

the bumblebees and no grasshoppers, beetles, or spiders for the millions of birds. And yet they have all come, across frozen rivers and open seas; from three mountain ranges, seven continents, and four oceans; and up from the depths of the frozen earth. Not only did they trust that summer would arrive, but also that their calving, breeding, nesting, and rearing grounds would be intact. I can't help but think how I lacked such trust for so much of the spring migration; how, in the face of blizzards and bears, such faith eluded us every day. Is it because we're human or because we've forgotten?

We had become part of something immense and immensely fragile. Behind every joyful moment lingered a kind of melancholy about the future, a dread that the two kinds of existence we'd experienced—the one in Kaktovik and the one on the calving grounds—would soon collide.

"We're smack-dab in the middle, aren't we?" asked Leanne as I gauged our position on the map. Indeed, the boundaries of the contentious 1002 lands—the unprotected, 1.5-million-acre parcel in the heart of Alaska's Arctic National Wildlife Refuge—were all around us. I traced an imaginary rectangle with my finger along the Arctic coast, then up the Canning River to the west of us, across the 1,000-foot contour of the foothills, and back down the Aichilik River. Leanne looked back out at the gamboling calves with a sigh.

"How much oil again?"

"Somewhere around 3.5 billion barrels," I reminded her, citing the U.S. Geological Survey's estimate of economically recoverable crude.

It sounds like a lot, but it is a mere drop in the bucket compared to rates of consumption. In 2002 the United States (which represents 5 percent of the world population but consumes 25 percent of the world's energy resources) gobbled up more than 7 billion barrels in a single year. In other words, the 27,000-year history of the caribou migration, as well as the livelihood of millions of birds, dozens of polar bears, and the entire Gwich'in culture were at risk of being annihilated for a six-month supply of oil.

"If every car increased its fuel efficiency by 1 mile per gallon, we'd save that much oil in ten years," I said, trying to lighten the despair that had descended on the tent. "If everyone kept their tires inflated to the proper pressure..."

"I know," interrupted Leanne. "If we had more wind farms. If we heated smaller houses. If we drove less. If, if, if."

She looked outside again as a calf sidled up to its mother and began to nurse, its nuzzling advances mirrored by dozens of others that came awake from their late-afternoon naps. Birds that had been quiet since late morning began singing as the light softened, seemingly confused about whether it was another day that was coming or simply another sunny night. Having slept much of the afternoon ourselves, we too felt disoriented, torn between two competing realities: one of timelessness, another of time running out.

There are three main reasons why the caribou go to Alaska's coastal plain to calve, and after a week of sitting, Leanne and I had observed each firsthand. First is the nutrient-rich forage. Believed by scientists to contain the highest protein content of any food found in the herd's range for that time period, the unique cotton grass that grows there turns half-starved mothers into milk factories for the rapidly developing calves (caribou's milk has the highest fat content of all land mammals'). Second is the lack of predators. The terrain is too wet and flat for wolves to dig dens and relatively unattractive to grizzly bears for unknown reasons, so the potential for a cow or her newborn to be hunted is less likely here than elsewhere. Indeed, after running into wolves and as many as four grizzly bears a day on the spring migration, Leanne and I had yet to see evidence of either animal on the coastal plain. Finally, a steady cool breeze off the Arctic Ocean delays the emergence of biting insects. While friends in Old Crow and other inland areas were already swatting at the year's first mosquitoes, Leanne and I sat with the tent doors wide open, dressed in short sleeves.

So what will change if oil development happens in the refuge? Would the caribou keep coming? And if not, would they survive?

In years when the majority of the caribou haven't reached the Arctic National Wildlife Refuge (because of deep snow, for example), calf mortality has skyrocketed (40 percent in the first month of 2001, for example, compared to the average 20–25 percent). And in years when some cows have calved in the refuge and others have lagged behind and given birth in the Yukon, some undeniable trends have emerged: calves whose mothers made it to the contested portion of the calving grounds enjoyed higher birth weights (presumably because of better nutrition) and lower rates of mortality (less predation) and maintained their size (and hence strength) advantage over cohorts born elsewhere.

But all this would be a problem only if caribou avoid areas of oil development—which the oil industry (and its political supporters) claims won't be the case. One of the oil lobby's favorite examples to support this claim is what happened to the Central Arctic Caribou Herd when the pipelines, compressor stations, and drilling rigs of the Prudhoe Bay development were built in part of their calving area almost two decades ago: the herd actually *increased* in size (from about 6,000 animals in 1978 to 23,000 animals in 1992).

But what the oil industry always leaves out of its argument are two very important points: first, where development encroached on traditional calving grounds, the cows abandoned the area; and second, because the coastal plain is much wider at Prudhoe Bay (100 miles versus only 20 miles in the refuge) and there are fewer animals there (23,000 caribou in the Central Arctic Herd versus 123,000 in the Porcupine Herd), there was somewhere for them to go. There is no alternative, high-quality calving area for the Porcupine Herd. In their case, displacement of the herd's calving grounds would mean a decline in the herd, perhaps even forcing them into extinction.

As the Alaskan and Canadian biologists who have studied the herd wrote in a strongly worded report prepared for the U.S. government in 2002: "State-of-the-art technology has not prevented displacement of calving from even the newer oil fields on Alaska's North Slope, and no proven technology exists that would ensure unrestricted passage through an oil field for the Porcupine Caribou Herd."

There were hundreds if not thousands of calves outside our tent now, but it was the one whose birth we'd seen that Leanne and I watched closely, tracking its remarkable development for the next four days. By the end of one day it was walking, on the second day it started hopping, and by the third day it discovered how to translate those hops into forward propulsion, launching itself after real and imaginary playmates in what barely passed as a run. Such a spectacle of self-discovery was amusing for Leanne and me, but not for its mother. No sooner had she found the exploring calf and resumed her almost constant grazing than the youngster was off again, necessitating a whole new round of grunts and head bobs to get it back. Gradually, after many such displays, a few scolds, and one or two charges from protective mothers that didn't appreciate its advances, the calf moderated its floppy-legged dashes and stuck closer to its mom. The all-important cow-calf bond was beginning to form.

A week of knocking elbows, rubbing shoulders, and poking one another with errant hands and clumsy feet had triggered another sort of bonding experience for Leanne and me inside the tent. Only it wasn't what I'd expected. We hadn't bickered, there were no complaints, and aside from the occasional joke, neither of us protested too loudly about the other's strengthening smells. Instead, something special had developed: a kind of shared consciousness that, more than anything, could be attributed to constant touch.

No matter what the time of day, parts of us were always pressed together—arm to arm as we crouched in the doorway taking pictures, head to leg as one kept watch and the other read, back to belly as we spooned together in the sleeping bag. The restlessness that had typified the first days of being surrounded were gone, and the claustrophobia we'd felt while tent-bound on the spring migration during storms hadn't returned. We still tossed, turned, fidgeted, and readjusted, but it seemed smoother and more coordinated—as though our personal rhythms had fused into a subconscious dance. We awoke well rested, spent our waking hours knowing what the other was thinking, and, as the days progressed, found less and less need to talk. The effect was magical: inside the tent all went quiet—and outside, as the cows and calves discovered their own system of body language all around us, the barks, grunts, bleats, and huffs that had dominated the last few days gave way to a soft, milling hush.

> *June 9—Jago River, Alaska*—Tonight while Leanne sleeps, I sit up and watch the calves arc around their feeding, resting mothers like a hundred new moons spinning around tired old suns. Orbits collide, reverse, and adjust themselves until suddenly one careens offtrack. Lost in the joy of movement, the calf charges right toward me, then suddenly realizes its mistake. It is the closest I have been to a caribou—4 feet—and as our eyes meet, a look of ages travels between us. Black pools of innocence, blue discs of uncertainty;

two species locked in the universal language of life. I try to think of what to do, how to act, but as soon as I do the moment is gone. The calf's legs quiver and in another instant it flees, leaving me alone, quivering as well.

Having endured the extreme moods of the Arctic for two months, Leanne and I knew it was inevitable that what seemed perfect would change. The next afternoon a grizzly bear walked over the rise and, within seconds, spread havoc over what had been a bucolic scene for seven calm days. A chorus of grunts and head-bobs rose up from the cows, calves ceased their games of tag midstride, and suddenly all the alarm signals, calls, and responses they'd been practicing all week were put to the test for the first time.

Despite the initial chaos, every cow-calf pair in the immediate area managed to unite and make its escape; but things were different for the handful of animals that had been across the river grazing on a small slope when the bear had appeared above them: nestled in a steep pocket below them was a 12-foot-high overhanging snowdrift that cut right across their escape route.

"Left. Way left," coached Leanne, as though the caribou looping to the edge and back again could hear her from 400 yards away. After a minute of trial and error, however, three of the cows found the narrow chute she was talking about and plunged down, half sliding and half running as their hooves skated through the soft snow. One by one, the rest of the half-dozen cows followed—but when it came time for the first calf to launch itself over the edge after them, the flow of animals stopped.

Unable to hold myself back, this time it was I who prodded them on.

"Get going!" I urged as two peered over the edge. Three hundred yards behind, the dark brown bear lumbered toward them, slowly closing in. Oblivious to what was coming, the calves froze as their mothers broke into a frenzy below them, huffing and barking while stamping circles in the snow. Unable to hold themselves back any longer, three of the cows charged back up the drift, punching a deep trench over the lip as they fought and churned their way to the top, scarcely pausing before nudging and then literally pushing a few of the calves over the edge with their muzzles, launching them down to safety in tumbling balls of wet fur.

It wasn't until we'd watched the whole group of them charge up the riverbank that we noticed one calf hadn't followed and was still looking for an alternate way down. There was no alternate way, of course, and as the seconds ticked past, the distance between the bear and the now-confused calf narrowed to just 100 yards.

"Oh no, this is exactly what the bear wants!" cried Leanne as the calf turned, sank up to its chest in soft snow, then pulled itself onto the adjoining tundra and climbed upslope instead of going down. Waving its nose in the air, the bear caught the calf's scent and followed it without quickening its pace. There was no reason to hurry; the separation had happened, and it was now just a matter of following the calf to its inevitable end. Weaving a little as it climbed, the calf stopped to look back one last time before cresting the horizon, then disappeared, with the bear ambling after it, slowly gaining with each step.

"Now what?" asked Leanne after a prolonged silence, but before I had a chance to respond, the caribou were answering her question, filing back from the direction they'd fled. With the bear gone, we were soon surrounded once again.

Although the bear hadn't been visible for long, its presence lingered as a kind of restlessness among the caribou. They'd come back, but their behavior had changed. Instead of settling into their old positions, they kept moving, circulating around us in a perpetual state of unease. When the cow that had escaped the snowdrift without her calf returned and began frantically searching, her lonesome calls exacerbated the herd's unrest. Some cows still fed, and a few of the calves still played, but it was all under a state of watchfulness and anxiety that hadn't been there before. Danger had introduced itself, and no matter how new life was, it would never be as innocent and carefree as it had been only an hour before.

Identifying individual animals under this new regime of movement proved confusing enough, but the fact that the cows had started shedding their antlers made the task virtually impossible. Except for the cow still calling across the river, we could no longer tell one animal from another, and the characters that had surrounded us for more than a week—the cow with one broken antler, the birth mother that had sported a picture-perfect rack—were gone, absorbed by the group identity of the herd. As a result, it was hard to know whether it was the same animals cycling around us or ones coming from elsewhere to replace those that had moved on.

When we woke from a nap, there was no questioning what had happened: only one animal was within view, and it was the calfless cow across the river. Hours had passed, and her calls had degenerated to hoarse, pitiful whispers that sent shivers up and down our spines.

Leanne tried to change the subject by pointing to the few brown specks climbing into the foothills almost 10 miles to the south. We both lowered our binoculars and looked at each other.

"This is the first time in eleven days we haven't been surrounded," she began. "Does this mean calving is over?"

I struggled to recall everything I'd read on the subject, then reached for my notebook and reread the report.

"Calving might be winding down, but they shouldn't be leaving," I responded. "It says they stick around in nursery groups until the bugs start to get bad at the beginning of July."

Leanne scrunched her nose and gestured toward the open door.

The screen wasn't up. Neither of us had seen a bug yet, aside from bumblebees, butterflies, and spiders.

"It's only mid-June. How do you explain what's happening now?" Leanne asked.

I stuffed the report back in the notebook and shoved it under the sleeping bag. I couldn't explain it. Nobody could. After a blissful ten-day reprieve on the calving grounds, we were now faced with all the same uncertainties, doubts, and pressures that had plagued us during the spring migration. This time, though, the stakes were even higher. According to everything I'd heard and read, the next phase of the migration was the most intense and dramatic, a time when groups of tens of thousands of cows and calves converge with large groups of bulls in massive postcalving aggregations and race into the mountains, covering as much as 30 or 40 miles a day. If we wanted the whole story of how valuable the calving grounds are to the caribou, then we needed to experience not only what they'd gone through to get there from their winter range but also what they would endure to get back.

"Tell you what," began Leanne when I failed to reply. "Let's wait until morning. If no caribou have shown up, we'll break camp and head for the foothills. If they have, we'll stay."

I mulled over her suggestion as I stared across the plain at those very foothills. A hint of green was creeping into the sloped folds and mounds that had been brown all week, and in the shimmering heat waves that rose off them, I struggled to focus on the distant dark dots. There was no hope of focusing, I soon realized, and no clear way of knowing which way the contorting, twisting shapes were headed or for how long. Unable to come up with a better plan, I agreed, but in my gut, I wondered whether tomorrow might already be too late.

With the rest of the afternoon ahead of us and no animals in the immediate vicinity, Leanne and I wasted no time getting out of the tent. Standing up was a luxury we hadn't enjoyed for more than a week, and we did so slowly, chortling as each vertebra straightened and slid into its rightful place.

"Tree," said Leanne, slipping into a yoga pose. While she stood balanced on one leg, I reached into the tent.

"The only one for miles!" I chuckled as I grabbed my socks and boots and came back out to sit beside her. While I did up my laces, she began what had been a daily routine before we'd left on the trip: the cobra pose, downward-facing dog, the child's pose, and others. With each position, her fingers and toes spread more deeply into the tundra, weaving themselves into the mat of creeping roots and blades of grass.

"See you in an hour," I whispered as I rose to my feet and blew her a kiss.

Not since the days before Kaktovik had I really used my body, and I strode off, relishing the feeling of pooled blood running back into my legs. But after twenty minutes of brisk travel, the pleasure graduated into a worrisome fatigue. Shaky and weak from a fortnight of sitting, I lay on the ground for a brief rest.

Lying there at eye level with the tundra, I noticed things that weren't obvious from a standing position: clumps of caribou hair were caught on the undersides of bushes, and beneath them, tips of bleached and moss-covered tines of old antlers barely poked from the ground. I'd seen dozens, if not hundreds, of the polished and blood-stained antlers that the cows had cast in the previous days, but these rough, half-buried specimens were a new discovery. Crawling on hands and knees, I made my way to the closest of the bunch and gently tugged it free. Roots, old caribou hair, and pellets of half-decomposed scat sloughed off the pock-marked surface, revealing the teeth marks where countless rodents had come to feed. I reached into the hole, trying to measure how much of the earth beneath me was hair and scat, but what I found was yet another well-preserved tine. I rolled onto my knees and scanned the surrounding sea of tussocks, feeling as though I was understanding the magnitude of the calving grounds for the first time.

How many antlers? I asked myself. How many layers? How much hair, scat, bone, and afterbirth? Buried how deep?

I thought of all the ways in which I'd heard the calving grounds described—Olaus Murie's "Garden of Eden," Roger Kaye's "Sistine Chapel," the Gwich'in's "Sacred Place Where Life Begins." And then I thought of the television clip I'd seen of Alaskan Senator Frank Murkowski on the floor of the U.S. Senate one and a half years before.

"This is what it looks like," he'd said, waving a sheet of blank paper during one of many prodevelopment pitches he'd made on Capitol Hill for the exploitation of the refuge. Frozen. Barren. Empty. "Nothing but snow and ice."

All the way back to the tent, I thought about development and what would happen if the drilling rigs were to arrive. Undoubtedly they would be staffed with engineers and experts from oil-rich places such as Texas and Alberta—people who understand the equipment but not the land. Same job, different place, they would joke, rubbing their hands in the chilly Arctic air.

But such a disconnect between one's actions and their effect is no joke, it's the problem. If the giant drill bit rips into the land here, it will be the gauges and dials they'll be watching, not the caribou parts and old birds' nests flying from the torn ground.

Two weeks on, two weeks off. Pockets stuffed full of money, they would fly home between shifts, not knowing what they'd done.

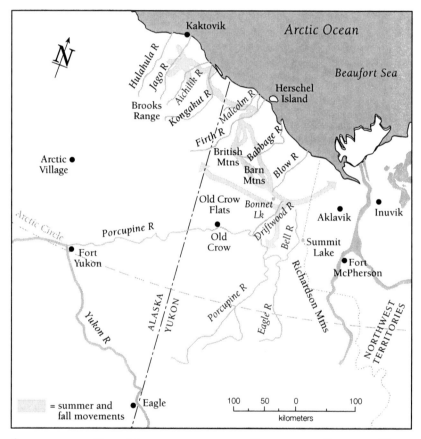

SUMMER AND FALL MOVEMENTS OF THE PORCUPINE CARIBOU HERD

post-calving aggregation

If you could enter their dreaming and dream with them deeply,
you would come back different to a different day,
moving so easily from that common depth.
—Rainer Maria Rilke, *Sonnets to Orpheus*, Part Two, XIV

The golden eagle dropped out of the sky like a knife, struck, then lifted with a strip off the calf's back. Bleeding and calling, the injured youngster took cover under its mother and the rest followed, twenty calves tucking under twenty cows as the brown shadow swooped in again. Muscles flinched, heads twisted, but the cows held their ground. Thwarted, the great bird flapped to a nearby hilltop and settled to eat what was clutched in its talons, knowing that if it waited long enough, it would soon have the rest. Unwilling to watch a calf bleed to death, Leanne and I continued on.

We knew to expect death. We knew that for every 100 calves born, an average of 25 die in their first month, but to witness it firsthand was shocking. A half mile later, however, the reality of this new phase of the migration began to sink in. I leaned down and gently prodded a waterlogged calf that had washed onto the shore of the Jago River.

"Drowned?" Leanne asked as I untangled the pretzel of tiny twisted limbs with a stick. I nodded and knelt down for a closer look, running my hand over the smooth hooves, the slender hip joint, the tiny muscles, and the wet, velourlike fur. The textures were everything I'd imagined: smooth, supple, and fresh. Releasing my grip, I let the wet carcass slip from my fingers, then stood up.

"It'll feed the bears," I assured Leanne.

"And the jaegers and ravens," she assured me right back. But no matter what we told each other, neither of us could quite absorb how quickly birth was usurped by death.

Three more carcasses—two untouched and one half-eaten—marked our route before we stopped at the base of the foothills and camped one last night along the Jago River. Tired and beaten from the two-day trudge across the coastal plain, we dumped our packs on the gravel bar, sat down, and rubbed our ankles and feet. The last hour had finally yielded a bit of elevation, and we had a view of the vast coastal plain for the first time. Glimmering gold and silver, the prairie of sedge dotted with shallow lakes looked deceivingly smooth.

"The walking looks good from afar, but it's far from good," quipped Leanne. I smiled but was too tired to laugh.

The traveling had been tricky—loose boulders along the river, with bogs of boot-sucking tussocks beside them—but it was the tracking that had been the biggest challenge. No caribou except the distraught mother had been in sight the morning we'd left the calving area, and with only an occasional snowdrift on the tundra, we hadn't had anything like a snow trench to suggest where to go next. Unlike in the spring migration, now the signs of where caribou had passed were subtle—a patch of trampled grass here, a sporadic line of hoofprints there—and we stopped frequently, bending down to decipher them in a muddle of signs left in previous weeks and years. It was ironic, but the best indication we had of being on the right track were the dead calves.

We knew we were closing in on a group when, instead of another muddy carcass, it was a live calf that lay on the tundra. I almost stepped on it before I saw it, a flash of fur that exploded from the lumpy ground before us, running, stopping, running, and then stopping again, confused as to whether it should approach or flee. I froze, water pooling around my boots as the dark saucer-size eyes latched onto me and the snub-nosed face gave a sniff. The same curious innocence of the calving grounds, tinged with loneliness and fear.

I scanned with binoculars for the mother but found no lone cow— no caribou at all—just a freshly churned trail meandering up the first gravel slope of the foothills three-quarters of a mile away. I stepped forward and waved, trying to usher the calf toward it, stopping when it bolted in the opposite direction, then waiting until it spun and returned, curious once again.

"I'm not your mother," I whispered.

The calf cocked its head, took a few steps forward, then circled back in front of the distant trail. Seizing my opportunity, I lifted my arms and ushered it forward for a second time.

It bolted this time, but not in the direction I'd intended. I lurched after it across the tussocks, trying to cut it off at a run. Arms waving, solar panel flapping, I winced as the 70-pound pack slammed and cut into my shoulders with every bouncing stride. Leanne shouted something unintelligible behind me, something about saving my energy, but I was possessed, the images of all the other carcasses playing through my head. Ditching my pack for one last effort, I pole-vaulted with my walking stick from tussock top to tussock top, my feet barely touching between bounds. Sensing my new speed, the calf shied and headed in the right direction, but success was short-lived. Accelerating, it veered into a tangent and didn't stop curving until it had doubled back. Defeated, I fell facedown, cursing as swamp water mixed with sweat.

"For Chrissake," I screamed after it. "You're going to die!"

The shout was loud enough to stop the calf, but not enough to bring it back. Looking at me one last time, it set off on its peculiar course, heading north instead of south, its legs swinging in a relaxed, loose-limbed gait. I took solace in its stride, imagining the calf finding safety in eternal movement, but when Leanne and I looked back a half hour later, a golden eagle circled where the calf should have been.

We found one more muddy carcass in the tussocks the next morning, and then it was all flowers, gravel, and hard ground as we climbed off the coastal plain and into the foothills. Following a whaleback of frost-shattered rock, we wove through spikes of purple lousewort, clusters of blue scorpion weed, and, wherever a little more soil had collected, the hardy stalks of yellow cinquefoil and pink cushions of arctic phlox. Using a network of freshly churned trails, we angled upward, treading on a fine layer of still-wet pellets smattered across the rocks.

Given the number of carcasses we'd stumbled across, the scene that greeted us at the first ridge top wasn't what we'd expected. Thousands of cows and calves grazed and played on either side of the shallow U-shaped valley before us, dwarfed by a line of peaks soaring skyward immediately behind. There was no rushing, no chaos, none of the disorder we'd imagined. If death was still lurking in the shadows, then it must have turned its attention somewhere else.

"Switch the caribou for sheep, and we'd be in New Zealand," marveled Leanne as she sat down and drank in the pastoral scene. I lowered myself beside her and watched as the closest calves nuzzled beside their feeding mothers, sampling a few willow buds and flowers before turning to play with those still cavorting behind. There was none of the tension that had followed the grizzly's visit to the calving grounds, and the restlessness that had pushed the animals into the foothills was suddenly gone. Aside from the change in scenery, it was as if the clock had run backward.

What had also changed was the cows' tolerance of our presence. When the various nursery groups collected themselves and began to drift east a few hours later, Leanne and I hesitated, hiding behind knolls and hollows, before daring to follow at a distance of a quarter mile. But such precautions proved unnecessary, we soon realized, for when we rounded a corner and surprised a group a half hour later, they showed none of the panic that had kept us tent-bound on the calving grounds. Although huffs and stamping hooves still announced our presence, and the closest of the cows assumed the usual wide-legged alarm stance, flight didn't follow. Now that the calves were three weeks old, there was no need for hypervigilance. All the days of playing, nursing, sleeping, and growing on the coastal plain had left the calves capable of outrunning a bear. Turning in unison, the group calmly walked off.

For the next four days, Leanne and I followed the caribou at a pace that was as close to effortless as we'd come yet. It wasn't the rush of the spring migration or the confinement of the calving grounds, but something in between. Walking enough to rid our joints of stiffness but not so much that our muscles tired, we seemed to find a flow that had eluded us until now. Free to cook, write, eat, and film outside the tent, we relished our new liberty, knowing that in another week or two, such luxuries would be a thing of the past. Indeed, the year's first mosquitoes—the big, slow-moving ones that had overwintered as adults—were just arriving, heralding the onslaught of their smaller, more ferocious counterparts that were about to emerge.

It was within this brief period of comfort that we saw our next grizzly bear, a medium-size bruin sporting a ring of silver hair around its brown chest and black shoulders, climbing 400 yards above the bench where we'd just finished pitching camp. Across the creek, between us and the bear, 100 caribou grazed and slept.

"Actually, there're two bears. No! Wait! Three bears," said Leanne. "Gathering around some sort of kill."

Reaching for my own binoculars, I watched the trio of blond and brown bears clamber up the slope to a giant bloodstain smeared across the hillside.

"Make that four," I said as a huge ursine head emerged from the red and brown carcass. Too big and dark to be a caribou, it was either a moose or musk ox that he was gorging himself on—which meant a meal of 500 to 800 pounds of meat. But despite the windfall, the big bruin wasn't willing to share. As the other three bears approached, he rose from the carcass and postured sideways, swinging his head and swatting the ground.

What the three smaller bears lacked in size they more than made up for in persistence, approaching and backing off so many times that finally the big bruin exploded from his meaty throne. Two fled, but the third darted in for a quick mouthful before scurrying off in the opposite direction, permitting the ravens to descend in a mob. Within seconds, the big bear was back, hopping onto hind feet for the last steps of its charge back to the carcass, swiping at the lifting curtain of black wings.

We watched for the next hour, cooking dinner as the drama unfolded two more times—bear chasing bears, bear chasing birds— with our eyes glued to binoculars as we ate. For all their efforts, however, the three smaller bears didn't succeed. Realizing he didn't need to go anywhere to protect his mother lode, the big bruin draped himself over the entire carcass and refused to budge. Leanne and I cleaned up, climbed into bed, and, after looking up one last time, closed the tent door and tried to get some sleep.

*June 15—Foothills of Brooks Range, Alaska—*Four bears lying on the mountain, two campers lying in the valley below, and in between 100 caribou bedded down, chewing their cud. Not too long ago, we wouldn't have thought twice about packing up and moving on.

But tonight, without discussion, we decide to stay. It's because of the bears' movements, because of the way the caribou hold themselves. Because of what they signal about intent and trust.

The wonderful flow we'd become a part of ended abruptly the next morning when I reached into the food bag and found only one breakfast and one dinner.

"Uh, Leanne?"

"Yeah?"

"What do you have for food in your pack?"

She reached in, pulled out a fist of empty plastic bags, rifled through them, and held up a lone fruit bar and a handful of nuts.

Before we'd left Kaktovik, Walt had grabbed our map and penciled in every place he thought he could land. There weren't many: one along the Jago River, the gravel bar where he'd originally picked us up along the Kongakut, and a spot between the two, where the Aichilik River left the foothills and spilled into a number of braided channels. At a distance of about 20 miles, the last was the closest. Unfortunately, it was off the trajectory of the caribou. Using my finger, I traced a route that would get us there: north through a gap in the foothills, then east along the bench of a steep hill, skirting the edge of the coastal plain.

"At least we'll see if any caribou are out there," said Leanne.

"Yeah, and tussocks," I lamented, silently berating myself. Lost in the pleasure of easy traveling, I'd let down my guard. We were already hungry; now, unless everything went perfectly, our food situation was going to get a whole lot worse.

The calm, clear weather of the past two weeks degenerated within hours of our leaving the caribou. After walking through the gap, we felt the wind wheel 180 degrees and pick up, slamming cold, wet air from the Arctic Ocean into our faces. Donning long pants, fleece jackets, wool hats, and rainproof anoraks, we turned to the east and bumbled into the fog.

"I don't think this is right!" shouted Leanne when a steep face of fractured rock reared out of the clouds two hours later. Veering left, we used the broken cliff as a guide, keeping it to our right as we skirted the ridge on a low bench.

For two days we traveled like that—half blinded by fog, with a shadowy mass of rock as a handrail; getting soaked, frozen, and iced over as waves of sleet, sun, snow, and freezing rain crashed in from the cold sea. Then, without our ever having seen the coastal plain or whether it held any caribou, the ground dropped away in front of us and the sound of rushing water filtered up through the clouds.

"The Aichilik!" shouted Leanne over the wind. Grabbing willow branches, stalks of fireweed, and any other available handhold, we slipped and slid down the muddy slope until another, very bizarre sound suddenly stopped us in our tracks. Craning our heads into the mist, Leanne and I looked at each other, shaking our heads.

"Human voices?"

Excited and a little nervous, we found the source of this new sound a few minutes after reaching the river, a cluster of colorful tents tucked into a swale of alder and willow bushes rimed with ice. After we yelled out a few shouts of "hello," a head popped up, followed by an arm that waved us to where seven people sat huddled under a tarp, backs to the wind.

"Where'd you guys come from?" asked the oldest among them, a weathered woman who, we later learned, had celebrated her seventy-third birthday the day before. Leanne glanced at me, not sure how to answer the question.

"The Jago River," I replied.

"Us too!" she exclaimed. "And where are you headed?"

Again Leanne looked my way, then jumped in. "We're not sure. Wherever the caribou take us."

Intrigued, the older woman invited us to join them. While we unclipped camera harnesses and wriggled out of pack straps, she and the others cleared stoves and pots to make space for us to sit.

Conversation was awkward at first, and we all spent a few silent moments sizing up each other and our equipment. It was strange to see people there, traveling like us, but so organized, composed, and clean. Their packs, which were smaller than ours, lacked the wires, regulators, and other video and solar paraphernalia that we had strapped to the outside of ours; their washed bowls, cups, and tightly packed meals were all freshly labeled; and unlike our own dirty pants, jackets, and shirts, their clothes' colors were still bright and radiant. The men were clean shaven, the women's hair light and fluffy; sitting next to them, Leanne and I couldn't help but feel a little rough.

After a round of introductions, the talk soon loosened and people shared what they did and where they were from. Helped by her teenage grandson, the older woman, Carol, was guiding the group of five middle-aged clients on behalf of the Sierra Club of California, leading a ten-day hike from the Jago to the Aichilik River valley and back again, just as she'd done for every one of the last thirteen years.

"We've come from all over the States for this," said one bundled-up man named Bill. "Hell, I drove from Chicago to Alaska. And when it's all over, I'm gonna have to drive back!"

"Chicago!" Leanne repeated. "How long did that take?"

"Oh, ten days, not including the two it took to buy and register a new car." He paused before explaining. "Hit a deer in Saskatchewan. Totaled my vehicle. But wouldn't let that ruin my trip. No sir! I've been dreaming and planning to come here all my life."

Others in the group gave similar testimonies. None had shared such misfortune en route, but all had gone to considerable effort and expense to experience what, in their words, was one of the last true wildernesses on earth.

"In the last five days we've seen four grizzlies, countless eagles, thousands of caribou, and a wolf taking down a calf," said one of the two women in the group.

"A wolf taking down a calf," I repeated. "We've been out for months and haven't seen that." The whole group beamed.

"You've been out for months?" checked Carol. "Gosh, you must be hungry!" Sifting through one of her group's food bags, she silently counted packets, then looked to the others for approval. "We're on a pretty tight food budget, but I think we can spare a couple of dried soups."

Everyone nodded.

While the water boiled, we talked more about what we'd seen and how it compared to Carol's past trips (colder this year, but one of the best for seeing caribou). Then, after a few more stories, talk turned to what always seemed to lurk behind such accounts of wilderness: the threats to it.

It was an appropriate topic, since the Aichilik River forms the eastern boundary of the contended 1002 lands. In other words, where we sat had one of two possible futures: it could soon be as busy as Prudhoe Bay with drilling rigs and pipelines, or it could become part of one of the largest internationally protected areas, contiguous with Canada's Ivvavik National Park and all the land between it and the opposite shore.

"Yeah, but what can we do about it?" asked the man closest to me. Before I could answer, someone else was talking about slide shows he planned to give to university students and community groups when he returned to Boston; another mentioned a possible magazine article; Leanne described the film she was shooting; Carol told about the hybrid vehicle she'd just bought. I talked about writing a book. It would all help, we agreed, but would it be enough?

With the soup ready, Leanne and I apologized for having nothing to offer in return but didn't mention how desperate our situation was.

We'd been really hungry for two cold, wet days, and all we had left was a quarter cup of chicken-and-rice dinner and a single fruit bar.

"We had an emergency a few years ago and had to cut the trip short and fly out of a place just downstream," said Carol after we explained we were there to receive a food drop. "It was a rough, makeshift strip, but it worked." She pulled out a dog-eared map and pointed to the gravel bar a mile downstream.

Thanking her and wishing everyone well, we set off to look for it, leaving behind the warmth of human company for another cold, foggy night.

Two days of waiting, and still no plane. With each passing hour, more and more of the reserves we'd gained in Kaktovik were slipping away.

We paced out what we thought was a workable landing strip—300 yards of washed cobbles that we marked with bits of orange garbage bag, scoured for sharp rocks and branches, and remeasured umpteen times. But the fog and wind were relentless, and after the fourth or fifth time, we stopped wasting our limited energy. Hungry to the point of feeling sick and dizzy, we savored the last few bites of the fruit bar, then tried to fall asleep to escape the hunger pangs.

The sound of an engine sent us rushing outside, searching, but one look at the ground-hugging cloud told us we'd been fooled again, first by the humming guy lines of the tent, then by one of our pack straps vibrating where it had snagged on a rock. The wind was making us crazy, eating at our nerves and driving us to frustration, ramming what seemed to be an endless supply of cold air and fog into the hills and our tent.

We called Walt on the satellite phone every morning and evening to give him a weather update. His tone remained chatty and bantering, but for us the humor of the situation had long passed.

"Well, what did you run out of food for?" he chortled across the airwaves after I'd explained tea bags were all we had left. There was a delay in the connection, a bit of static, but in the background I could hear voices and the bubble of the deep fryer.

> *June 18—Aichilik River, Alaska*—The blissful timeless-ness we felt with the caribou only 20 miles back has given way to another painful wait. There is a trend here, a deterioration from belonging to loneliness each time we leave the caribou for a food drop. The blizzard at Bonnet Lake, the storm along the Firth River, the decision to go into Kaktovik, and now sitting here in this cold, forsaken wind. Each time our dependence on the outside world surfaces, conditions deteriorate, and a foothold to some alternate reality slips away. We are trying to be caribou but are continually pulled back by our modern human needs. Four days ago, it was all about the caribou and sunshine that surrounded us; now it is the future we're focused on and whether or not that plane will get in.

I had a small spool of fishing line in the bottom of my pack, and the next morning I set off to where the braided Aichilik collected in a deep pool. I had grown up fishing, but it was always for sport, not survival. Now, as I tied on the fly and a small rock, a deadly seriousness took hold of me. Knowing it could mean the difference between going to bed full or hungry, I double-checked every knot, then threw it in.

Within seconds the first tug came up the line, and I instinctively jerked it back, pulling a 2-pound arctic grayling to the surface in a series of flashing and flaring iridescent colors until I'd landed it on the bank. I lunged after it, pouncing on its cold, hard muscle, clubbing it hard and too many times as the fanlike dorsal fin twitched in the cleft of my fingers then went quiet. Blood oozed from the gills, a few eggs passed out the hind end, and a smattering of scales drifted back into the water, spinning downstream in tiny rainbows of glittering light.

The wind died as we were licking our fingers and tossing the bones into the fire, and by the time the bones had burned, the blanket of low-lying clouds had rolled back and disappeared. Shedding jackets, wool hats, and long underwear, we basked in the warmth that flooded behind it, pulling out the sleeping bag, pads, journals, clothes, cameras, lenses, and everything else that was moist and damp inside the tent. The heat was wonderful, but it was the silence we cherished. No tent flapping. No wind roaring past our ears. For the first time in days, Leanne and I talked in whispers instead of shouts.

The plane came early that evening, a drone that this time really was an engine, a far-off dot growing until it was the familiar black-and-white Cessna, dipping above us to look over the makeshift runway, then banking hard before touching down in a spray of gravel and rocks. Drifting past our last marker, Walt hit the brakes hard, pitching the plane onto one wheel to bring it to a stop before nosing into a steep ditch.

"Strip's short!" he barked, climbing out and storming off to roll a few of the larger rocks out of the way to turn around. Too hungry to care about his brusque greeting, Leanne and I wasted little time in pulling open the passenger door and delving into the boxes sitting on the backseat. When I opened the grease-stained one and found two Waldo burgers wrapped in tinfoil, my difficulty with Walt's gruff ways suddenly eased.

"Thanks," we called out between mouthfuls. Walt gave a half-hearted wave while he kicked rocks and moved branches 50 yards away.

"So you're happy now?" he asked, returning ten minutes later to help us unload the last of the boxes. The burgers were gone and we were already into the candy bars. Seeing our faces streaked with ketchup and chocolate, he managed a smile.

"Well, gotta get going," he said, already climbing back into the cockpit. "Lots of people waiting for flights back at the hotel."

"Wait!" I dropped what I was eating and ran to the pilot's window as he flicked switches and checked dials. "What did you see on the way in? Any caribou?"

He stopped midway through his preflight checklist, pausing in thought.

"You know, it's a weird year. Hardly any animals on the coastal plain—just a few dozen. But there are thousands in the hills and mountains."

"Where?" I asked, but Walt was writing numbers in his notebook, checking and rechecking his watch. "Which direction?" I pressed.

"Oh," he said, looking up. "Let me think. At least as far back as the Jago River, and east to the Canadian border. In the hills and pretty spread out."

"And the calving grounds?" It felt as if I was trying to squeeze water from a stone. "Any news from the biologists about where the majority of the cows calved?"

"Oh yeah," he apologized, "I never thought to tell you. One of the Fish and Wildlife guys came to the hotel for a meal the other day. According to him, they were concentrated right along the base of the foothills between the Hulahula and Aichilik rivers." He chuckled as he watched me try to recall where the Hulahula was located. "Let me put it this way," Walt continued. "From what the helicopter pilot told me, it sounds like where he dropped you ended up being the heart of it all."

Thanking him, I stepped back as he taxied away.

"What are you looking so smug about?" Leanne asked once the wings flashed overhead and the buzz of the engine disappeared.

Not only had we been smack-dab in the center of the herd on the calving grounds, I told her, but if everything Walt had said was true, a short walk into the foothills would position us perfectly once again.

Buckles sang under the tension; seams stretched. We were at capacity—beyond capacity—with cheese, salami, and other food swinging from plastic bags tied to our packs.

The decision to have Walt bring in two food caches instead of one had seemed like a good one while we'd been stuck in the fog waiting and hungry. The caribou would be aggregating and rushing into the mountains by the time we'd need another one, we reasoned, and the last thing we'd want was to have to stop, wait, and be thwarted by poor weather yet again. And so we'd asked Walt to deliver twenty-eight days' worth of food instead of the usual fourteen. The result was that each of us now had to carry well over half our body weight—70 pounds for Leanne, and 90 pounds for me.

Finding caribou helped take our minds off the pain. Just as Walt had predicted, we crested the first foothill and there, in the dip of the next small valley, half a dozen nursery bands of a few hundred animals each lay scattered across rolls of blooming flowers and greening grass. We sat down and watched for a few minutes, enjoying the sun and the view of mountains just beyond as calves zipped and tore around in circles, stopping beside their mothers every few minutes to bump and tug at their udders while the cows dozed and grazed. Helping one another back up, we hunched our loads back onto our shoulders, tightened our hip belts, and merged into the slow-moving procession of animals, feeling as though we'd joined the migration right where we'd left off.

For the first few hours, everything did seem the same, but as the day wore on, we began to notice subtle differences. It was partly visual: the cows looked even more disheveled than the week before, their coats a patchy mix of new and old hair, and the calves—which were noticeably larger—were changing color, their fuzzy, reddish-brown birth coats turning a sleek, silvery gray. But it was more than that. Something about how they moved was different, a faint urgency that hadn't accompanied our earlier days in the foothills. Instead of gently drifting, they were moving with purpose and direction. In the four days that had passed since we'd last seen the caribou, our pace had slowed and theirs had quickened.

By the end of that first evening, the occasional group passed us at a trot. We followed them as best we could, grinding to the low pass over which they disappeared, reaching the top in time to see them as specks on the floor of the next valley. They slowed for a while, spread across the floodplain like dispersing seeds, but before we were halfway caught up, they drew together and moved again, slipping up and over the next hill with a grace that belittled our own hitching gait. After fording the shallow river, we helped each other off with our loads and collapsed.

"We need to keep going."

"What?"

"Something's up," I insisted. "Something's changing. The caribou are really starting to move."

"How can we?" Leanne huffed, kicking at her pack. "Besides," she said a few seconds later, "I doubt they're going far." She looked at the rounded ridge 500 feet above us, one of many we'd climbed and descended all day. "We'll find them tomorrow," she assured me. "In the next valley."

I wanted to believe her, but by the time we finished eating, brushing our teeth, setting up the tent, and climbing into bed, enough groups had passed for me to know she was wrong. Indeed, after we packed up and staggered to the top of the rise the next morning, the only animals still in view were those that had passed us while we'd cooked breakfast an hour before.

I said nothing about my growing worry, convinced that Leanne would soon reach the conclusion that, to me, seemed so obvious:

regardless of how heavy our packs were and how little food we'd survived on for most of the previous week, we needed to find extra energy from somewhere and move farther each day. If we didn't, we wouldn't have any animals to follow at all. But after our customary eight hours of walking, she dropped her pack, let out a sigh, and began working through the chore of setting up camp.

"You're not seeing it, are you?"

Leanne stopped fiddling with the tent and looked across at me, squinting in the late-afternoon light.

"Seeing what?"

"The change," I said, feeling a ball of frustration tightening in my chest. "The energy. The migration ramping up."

Leanne threw me a blank look.

"C'mon," I continued, trying to keep a steady, calm voice. "You can't tell me you haven't noticed! All day they've been running. Racing! Hardly stopping to feed." I waited, but she said nothing. After a few moments, she turned and continued with the tent, then set up the stove and pulled out a meal. Grabbing the pot and water bag, I stormed off to the creek.

An hour later, while eating dinner, I broached the subject again. Part of me—the part that cherished the intimacy we'd shared on the calving grounds and ever since—said to let it be. But another part couldn't let it rest. After months of separating our days into equal parts walking, eating, and sleeping, we were at a turning point, and if being caribou was our goal, then something had to give.

"We've talked about this from the beginning," I began. "A time when the caribou will race for the mountains and there will be no rest, no stopping, no time to do anything but try to keep up. We're going to have to accept hunger, deal with the exhaustion ..."

"Going to?" Leanne interrupted. "We already are!" She was laughing as she said it, making fun of my effort to rally the troops.

"I'm serious!" I barked. "Remember what we read in all the reports?

Remember what the biologists told us? One day they're scattered for miles; the next, they're headed for the mountains in groups of ten or twenty thousand. This could be it—the beginning of the postcalving aggregation. If we don't move now, we'll miss everything."

Leanne crinkled her nose and shook her head.

"It's too early. There's barely a mosquito or fly around. What you're talking about happens in mid-July, not the third week of June."

Just then, another fifty cows and calves appeared on the slope behind us, splitting into two smaller groups that splashed across the creek before charging off. I pointed to where they'd cantered behind a small hill.

"Who's to say it can't happen earlier? Who's to say it isn't happening now?" I paused, waiting for Leanne to answer as I gathered my thoughts. "We have to follow caribou even if it doesn't suit us. We have to give up our comforts. Give up our schedules. Move if they're moving—right now!"

Leanne looked over her shoulder at the departing caribou, then down at the ground, but not at me. She was hurt by those last comments. They didn't even begin to acknowledge all she'd already endured while filming the whole time: the blizzard, the bears, the ice-fringed rivers and creeks crossed in bare feet. Yet something kept me pushing, an obsession that had resurfaced and, in that moment, overpowered all feelings of love, admiration, and respect.

"Remember what we told reporters? How we said we'd walk through the night no matter how tired we were? How we would take down the tent at a moment's notice in a bid to keep up? That time is here, Leanne. It's staring us in the face. We have to try."

"But Karst," she pleaded, "I'm exhausted, and it's 11:00 PM."

"Haven't you heard anything?" I shouted, no longer holding back. "The caribou don't care what time it is, and neither should we if we're serious about keeping up!"

I eased off once her tears began to flow, but it was too late. Curling into the tundra, Leanne began to sob, pushing me away each time I tried to console her. I stood back and watched her whole body heave as months of frustration and anxiety poured out. There was something inside me that wanted to cry like that too, some dark hole where so much stress and uncertainty had collected. But nothing came out.

By 6:00 AM, the trickle of animals we'd started off with at midnight was a half-mile-wide front of caribou many animals deep. We were eastbound, less than 3 miles from the Kongakut River, and we endeavored to outrun them, trying to extend what was already a day-and-night marathon by another few hours. But even if we had been fresh, we couldn't have done it; the entire slope behind us had darkened with animals that were racing toward us like the shadow of a fast-moving cloud.

I grabbed Leanne and pulled her down into the tussock beside me, and we exchanged grins as she gave my hand a squeeze.

The tension and anger from our earlier argument had fallen away once we'd started moving again, first loosened by the rhythm of walking and then in the exciting rush of caribou that had only continued to build through the night. But it wasn't just caribou we'd noticed. We'd soon forgotten our differences and had felt the tiredness strangely dissipate as well. Like a couple of teenagers who'd broken their curfew, we reveled in details that, until then, we hadn't noticed because of our dutiful concession to scheduled sleep. How the upland sandpipers circled over our stretched-out shadows. How the caribou seemed much calmer. And how the long-tailed jaegers that normally dive-bombed and forced us into tiresome detours simply watched as we stumbled past their camouflaged nests. There was a magic afoot at night that wasn't there in the daytime, a calmness and clarity that affected the animals and us. It was partly the soft, golden light, but it was more than that. Not just vision but all our senses somehow seemed heightened. We had moved beyond tiredness toward something else.

"Shush," I whispered as Leanne rustled in the grass beside me. I waited until she was quiet, then waved a finger toward the oncoming herd. "You hear it?" It was unmistakable this time, the same kind of sound I'd heard near the end of the spring migration, but stronger now. Not hooves drumming—though there were those too—but something deeper, some infrasonic resonance on the edge of human hearing, humming an oscillating song. I closed my eyes and felt it spread through my body.

"They're thrumming," I said quietly.

Not only was Leanne awake this time, but to my relief she heard it too. "It's coming from there *and* there," she whispered while pointing to either side of where the front of animals had split. But before I could confirm it, the sound was gone, buried in the chaos of snorts, huffs, and tendon clicks as the nearest animals closed in.

We tucked ourselves into the tundra as deeply as possible, waiting as they splashed down the creek for the final few hundred yards, but it wasn't deep enough. The lead cow spotted us and flinched, and a reactionary wave passed through the herd. Detouring instead of moving right over us, they passed 150 yards away.

"More coming," I predicted a few minutes after the last animal had passed. Leanne turned her head as the gamy scent of urine and warm flesh settled over us, listening for the renewed thrumming as a tuft of caribou hair parachuted into her lap. Then, like the next wave of an advancing army, silhouettes appeared on the western horizon, descending, and we were overtaken once again.

"C'mon," I said, reaching for my pack. But my newfound energy had limits, and this time when I grabbed the shoulder strap, the load didn't budge. Swooning as she stood, Leanne didn't even bother picking up her pack before staggering to the nearby creek. Finding a soft gravel bar there, we stomped the caribou prints flat, pitched the tent, and promptly fell asleep.

We didn't sleep long—only three hours—before we were up again, pulled awake by heat. Baking in the midday sun, the tent was like a greenhouse, and I opened the door wide for air.

"Caribou?" croaked Leanne.

The light was harsh, nothing like the velvet textures of the night before, but after a few seconds a washed-out shape moved across the valley. With the new search image established, I quickly spotted a hundred more. I felt a twitch run down my legs. Without waiting for an answer, Leanne rustled out of the sleeping bag and immediately began to pack.

For the next four days we continued without routine or pattern, napping for two or three hours, walking for eight or nine, resting for one or two more before moving yet again. Pushed by the caribou, we fooled our bodies into doing more with less. We wolfed down dinner in the morning, scooped in handfuls of nuts or skipped lunch altogether, and paused for quick breakfasts in the middle of the night. Tired and confused, we moved beyond nagging hunger, beyond the blunt edge of exhaustion, beyond the limits of each day before. Awash in caribou, we came upon entire drainages—the Kolakut, the Kongakut, the Palokat, the Clarence, unanticipated and unnamed until we later looked at the map. The last of the ice shelves, the first of the flowers, the endless creeks, passes, and swamps melded in a blur of rushing bodies, wild-eyed dashes, and fresh trails. No longer did we know where we were or where we were going; caribou became our existence. Scat, hair, and the heavy scent of running, racing animals infiltrated everything—our clothes, our sleeping bag, our food, and the water we gulped down in great handfuls from the creeks. Dizzy and disoriented, we found that old boundaries began to blur, and the caribou that had dominated one realm of consciousness slipped into another, occupying our dreams.

It first happened somewhere near the Alaska-Yukon border, after we'd half-jogged through another night and set up the tent to nap while our boots, pants, and socks hung on the surrounding bushes to dry. Two hours later, everything was dry and stiff in the hot sun.

"A bull," I whispered through cracked lips as Leanne came awake in the sweltering tent beside me. Tiny beads of perspiration clung to her weather-beaten face.

"A what?" she croaked, lifting the bandana from her red, swollen eyes.

"I dreamt we saw our first bull."

She blinked, trying to get her bearings in the twenty-four-hour sunlight, then waited. It wasn't normal for me to remember my dreams, much less talk about them, and she listened intently as I described the scene: a rocky hill in the foreground, a green slope behind it, and a lone, velvet-antlered bull walking between the two, following a boulder-strewn ridge. She nodded after I finished, then yawned as she opened the door.

The next second she was wide-eyed and fully awake.

"You're not going to believe this," she said, unable to contain her excitement as she pointed out the door.

There, across the valley, walking through the exact scene I'd described, was the first bull of our trip.

> *June 25—Clarence River, Alaska*—There is no explain-
> ing this, no room for the old skepticism and doubt.
> And although a part of me still wants to question—to
> know exactly how and why—it is smaller than before,
> a voice that's scarcely audible amid the overwhelming
> urge to surrender and accept. It is the act of moving
> that has brought me here; the work of being caribou:
> the miles, the weather, the bears, and the uncertainty,
> hammering every extraneous thought, action, question,

phone number, and song from my head. Cleansed, I am on the edge of something, some other realm of knowing, being pushed and pulled through the same physical world but in a different dimension of space and time.

The lone bull heralded the arrival of many more behind it, a parade of antlers that slid seamlessly into the rushing groups of cows and calves. Much to our surprise, there were no greetings or other hints of joyful reunion. Without so much as slowing down, the cows streamed onward, leaving the bulls no choice but to trot after them, turning from their slow, northward ramble to take a new, hurried eastward tack.

Next to the emaciated cows, the taller and heavily muscled bulls fairly swaggered, and their fat bellies were all the evidence Leanne needed in order to assume that, as usual, it was the females who were getting the raw deal. While the cows had half-starved themselves to get to the calving grounds, give birth, and provide milk for the calves, the bulls had been living the easy life, slowly ambling north after the hard work was done. Knowing better than to aggravate Leanne's feminist leanings, I kept my admiration for their huge, antlered presence to myself.

Although it didn't influence the direction of the herd's movement, the bulls' arrival did bring a new calming energy that hadn't been present before. It was as though their larger size held a confidence that spread to every animal within view. The wild-eyed dashes that had typified so much of the previous days' rush dissipated as more and more males infused the ranks, and so there were fewer separations, fewer abandoned calves. There was still a hurry, but it was no longer frantic, and after we waded a knee-deep river, we climbed to the top of the next knoll to find a group stopped and feeding for the first time in days. Following their cue, we dropped our packs.

"That was the Backhouse River," I said, pulling out the map. Leanne looked down as I penciled in our route, crossing back and forth over the faded line that marked where we'd skied north that spring. There were a few loops and doglegs, but together the two routes depicted a remarkably direct journey into Alaska's Arctic National Wildlife Refuge and back into the Yukon's Ivvavik National Park.

"We crossed back over the Yukon border yesterday!" marveled Leanne after I'd plotted our recent progress. Indeed, in four intense days of walking, we'd covered what had taken more than a week on skis. I looked north toward the ocean, then south into the mountains, trying to remember how everything that was green and shimmering now had looked back then. It had been foggy and snowy, of course. What we'd thought were imposing mountains were, in fact, benign hills, and the deep, iced-over river we'd fearfully skied across was now no more than a glorified creek.

"How could we have been such fools?" I wondered aloud.

Leanne scoffed after I'd shared my insights, lying back as she opened her arms and embraced the sun. "The weather was different," she reminded me. "And don't forget all the bears."

I nodded, amazed at how our attitudes had changed. The bears were still out there, still potentially dangerous, but the foreboding that had surrounded us then was gone. Through constant exposure, we'd learned to live with the fear.

Leanne pointed north to where the wide, white lens of the Arctic Ocean dropped off the horizon. "Now there's something that looks the same."

She wasn't exaggerating. Despite weeks of effort, the sun hadn't made much headway, pushing just a tiny fretwork of narrow, blue open-water leads into an otherwise still-continuous skin of ice.

We tried napping, but no sooner had we set up the tent than we were dealing with a problem that would plague us on every calm, sunny day for the rest of our trip: inside, it was too hot to sleep, and outside it was too busy with bugs. Leanne and I adopted opposing strategies, with identical results: she stripped naked and sweated inside; I piled on clothing and lay drenched and sleepless outside on the ground.

We were groggy with tiredness and heat exhaustion when we set off again, but those feelings passed as we walked deeper into the night. The simple salve of moving helped, yet it was the dropping sun that made the difference, turning what had been harsh, blown-out afternoon light into a long and rapturous twilight. Traversing the ridge to a low saddle, we bid adieu to the ocean and slid into the Fish Creek valley, where groups of caribou, a lone grizzly, and a band of Dall sheep splashed across the shadows in brushstrokes of fiery light. Muscles twitched in the smoky sunshine, velvet antlers blazed, and after hesitating for just a moment, we assumed our place in the glittering scene feeling something spark inside us as well: a vague memory of belonging, perhaps, or a deepened faith in the world.

Regardless of what it was, a shift had happened: the tortoise-and-hare race we'd had with the caribou in the spring was over; competitors had become companions. With the sheep watching from a ridge, we took our position in the parade of animals, following caribou followed by the grizzly, sharing the same challenges and fears.

A deep furrow of fresh tracks led south up the gravel bars toward the mountains, but across the Malcolm River, a group of animals climbed into the next row of foothills, continuing east. Leanne and I looked at the deep, chalky water and shuddered. Favoring the choice of the path of least resistance over the unwritten rule of following animals rather than tracks whenever possible, we turned toward the mountains, avoiding what looked to be a difficult ford.

It was the first in a series of mistakes that would haunt us for weeks, breaking not just the 100-mile flow of animals since the calving grounds but the flow that had developed inside us as well. After walking upriver for an hour, I turned to Leanne, feeling something wasn't right.

"Why don't we have a sleep and see what happens?"

Leanne looked upstream to where the wide outwash plain we were following narrowed and disappeared into the angled peaks of the British Mountains. At 4,000 feet above sea level, they aren't quite the towering summits of Alaska's Brooks Range, but they looked formidable nonetheless. Steep slopes of loose, shattered rock dropped into a shallow canyon, and behind it a craggy skyline rose in a series of high passes guarded by broken cliffs. We were already dizzy and weak from trying to keep up with the caribou through the foothills, and the prospect of rushing headlong into the mountains wasn't appealing.

I don't know what I expected to happen there on the bank of the Malcolm, but when a mass of animals rounded the corner just as we were waking from our midafternoon nap, I couldn't help but interpret it as a sign.

"Is that real?" I asked, still foggy with sleep. An entire hillside was moving from the coastal plain toward us, shape-shifting in the last of the day's heat waves, tracking toward the mountains through ribbons of shadow and light.

"This is it," said Leanne as still more animals rounded the corner. It was the most we'd ever seen together, and she was beside herself, practically jumping as hundreds more caribou pressed into what was already a seething, shimmering mass.

I nodded, sharing her excitement. Everything seemed to be lining up for a postcalving aggregation: the weather, the animals, the emerging bugs. After a week of half-killing ourselves, we were about to reap the reward of not only witnessing but becoming a part of a gathering of unfathomable force.

But that wasn't what Leanne meant.

"This is it," she repeated, almost squealing as she pointed, turned, and pointed again. "That mountain, the hillside … everything! Even the light."

I looked at her as a gust of wind hit, squinting as grits of sand and seeds blew past in a whirlwind of dust. She reached out with both hands and grabbed my shoulders, laughing as she gave me a hug, then a shake.

"I swear this is what I just dreamed!"

"Dreamed?" I asked. "When?"

"Just now!" Leanne enthused, pointing back to where we'd taken down the tent ten minutes before. "During our nap."

There were no further questions from me this time, no skeptical looks or doubtful remarks, but what did surface in the swirl of building potential was an old weakness: for the first time in weeks, I speculated on what might happen next.

It was in that moment of looking forward—of imagining a scene even more dramatic than the one unfolding around us—that everything began to go wrong.

"There's a pass ahead," I shouted to Leanne, remembering it from a spring patrol I'd made as a park warden two years before. "It's steep," I admitted, recalling how we'd had to pack the final snow slope on foot before getting the snowmobiles over, "but it's a shortcut to where the Firth River and Sheep Creek meet."

From the look Leanne gave me, I knew I didn't need to say anything more. The stretch of incised canyons and white-water ledges where the two drainages converge had an almost mythical status among park staff and visitors, a place where more caribou trails converge than anywhere else in the already spectacular 100-mile-long valley. In fact, Leanne had been one of those visitors on a rafting expedition with me two years earlier; she remembered not only the trails etched in the canyon walls but the stories I'd told of the time I watched hundreds of bulls plunge into the frothing water the month before. For a week afterward, Parks Canada had closed the river to all human traffic, allowing the eighteen grizzlies that had converged on the dozens of carcasses enough time and space to eat and move off.

"How far?" Leanne asked, her thoughts jumping ahead like mine. She was already lifting her pack as she posed the question, and I reached down for mine, struggling to recall the route. One pass. A steep climb to get up and over it. About 20 miles.

Some of the best wildlife encounters of the entire trip occurred over the next few hours—a wolverine loped within yards of us, and we passed within a stone's throw of a lone musk-ox bull—but they scarcely registered. Even a grizzly bear and a surprisingly deep crossing of the Malcolm River did little to distract us from our new mission of getting to the Firth before the caribou did. Hardly caring whether the bruin noticed us, we gave it only a 200-yard berth and pushed past as it dug roots and flipped rocks; then we stepped into the water, not stopping to reconsider when the cold, swift current climbed past our navels and lapped at our chests. We made the ford, then walked—even hitched in a half-jog at times—and kept moving, our clothes drying on our bodies as we made our way up the main valley. After finding the mouth of the small tributary that led toward the Firth River, we turned left and began to climb.

Within an hour of leaving the spot where Leanne had recalled her dream, we lost sight of the mass of caribou, but the image of her vision stayed fresh in our minds, driving us harder upward. Almost twelve hours passed, and not a single animal materialized behind us, but we didn't give it a second thought. We were happy, in fact, for the longer the animals fed or rested behind us, the more time it gave us to position ourselves for the drama we were so sure was about to unfold. From memory, I already had the spot picked out: a high prow of rock that jutted into a corner of the twisting river canyon, a perfect lookout over the entire valley, with a flat, grassy bench above it that would accommodate the tent. We were set.

When we arrived on the shore of the Firth River, everything was as I'd imagined—the campsite, the lookout, the frothing crush of white water; the only ingredient missing was caribou. Cameras and tripod at the ready, and with a good supply of batteries, film, food, and water neatly arranged around us, we settled in for what we thought was going to be a very short wait.

Minutes passed. Hours. And then a day.

"They're not coming," I blurted, finally saying what was on both our minds. After we'd sat up half a day and a whole night, the only animals we'd seen were the bold ground squirrels that, after chewing a hole in one of our food bags, were making moves toward the tent.

"Oh c'mon, Karst," said Leanne, polishing the lens of her video camera for the third or fourth time in as many hours. "Give it a chance."

I shook my head. "No. They'd be here by now. We screwed up."

After another day of waiting, Leanne finally agreed.

During the two days that followed, we climbed onto the surrounding ridges and limestone towers in the hope a miracle would happen and even a handful of caribou might come, but with each new vista we grew more disenchanted. Hundreds of miles of caribou trails stretched like spokes of a wheel in all directions, but not a single animal was in sight.

> *July 1—Firth River, Yukon*—Canada Day, and we find ourselves in the most Canadian of places. Awe-inspiring cliffs of orange and gray limestone lift from the slopes around us, and below, the deep green water of the Firth—the same river that will teem with thousands of arctic char in another month—carves ever deeper into a canyon whose shady recesses still hold winter jewels of aqua blue ice. But neither Leanne nor I are celebrating, for without the wild energy of

the caribou, birds, bears, and other life that comes with them, this is a lonely and empty place. It feels haunted—I feel haunted, like the time when I was a kid and my schoolteacher held up a historic picture of the plains covered with bison.

Late on the second evening of waiting, and on the tail end of another series of short walks, I hung back to visit an archaeological site I knew from my days as a park warden while Leanne returned to the tent. Piles and circles of lichen-covered rocks lay where hunting drive lanes, tent rings, and stone hearths had once overlooked the Firth River, strategically positioned to corral and confuse the caribou that had been pushed there by some hunters while others waited with their spears, hidden just below the canyon rim. I walked from one remnant to the next, reached down and examined a bone fragment that had been exposed by the wind, then put it back, feeling the heft of thousands more in the mat of roots and soil beneath it.

I couldn't remember the age of the site. It was of coastal Inuit lineage—either Thule or Dorset—although the Gwich'in and other inland Athapaskans had used the valley as a trading route. Such details didn't matter to me. What did was the feeling of sitting there and imagining the lives that had been lived. Unlike Leanne and me, those people had been tied to the movements of the caribou for a lifetime, not a simple months-long trip. In stark contrast to our own situation, they had no safety net of food drops, a satellite phone, a solar panel, or planes to back them up. When they made a mistake, the consequence often was death.

Sitting there in that same landscape with the same goal—trying to find caribou—I couldn't help wonder about the intensity and spirituality of these ancient people, the power and strength of their existence when being caribou wasn't what hung in the balance, but being alive. What dreams and visions had they experienced? What gateways had been opened to what worlds? And then there was the thrumming. Having spent every minute outside, they couldn't not have heard it, but how had it moved them? How had they incorporated it into the deeper wisdom that guided their lives?

Standing up, I walked back to the pylons of rock from the old drive lane and stood near the edge of the canyon, drinking in a scene that probably hadn't changed much in hundreds of years. The Firth River still hammered past in a crush of white-water holes and standing waves, slapping at the caribou trails that still funneled down wherever the rock walls provided an inch of room. I imagined caribou swimming it, Native hunters swimming it, and then us.

Shivering with the thought, I took a few more steps to an inviting hollow and plunked down in a sun-warmed nest of grass. It was the perfect spot—out of the wind, just out of sight of the nearby drive lane, and shaped in a way that fit every curve of my legs and hips. Hunkering down, I settled in to do what every person—Gwich'in, Inuvialuit, or otherwise—had done here before me:

I sat and waited, hoping caribou would come.

summer
wandering

Be. And, at the same time, know what it is not to be.
That emptiness inside you allows you to vibrate
in resonance with your world. Use it for once.
— Rainer Maria Rilke, *Sonnets to Orpheus*, Part Two, XIII

R eady?"
No answer.

"Ready?" I shouted. This time Leanne snapped alert from where she stared, mesmerized by the current. Swallowing hard, I double-checked the rope and, clenching one end in a trembling hand, stepped in.

Cold stabbed at my feet as I angled upstream, staying on the slow and easy side of the boundary between shallow and deep water. But after I'd taken half a dozen steps, the submerged alluvial fan of Sheep Creek abruptly ended and the real river—the one that whips caribou to their death and carves canyons from stone—began. Hesitating at this line that separated the two, I looked across the surge of spitting, popping water and waited for another wave of nausea to pass. It wasn't

175

that far, I reassured myself, looking to the cliffs on the other side. It wasn't impossible. Taking a deep breath, I leapt toward it, arms cycling through the air.

I had a good idea of how I wanted to do it, of how I wanted to jump that first seam of white water and land on my belly to surf the leading wave, but no sooner did I hit the ripping current than there was no way of knowing what was happening. A brief skipping sensation gave way to a sinking feeling, and then there was nothing but the shock of cold water. It was pressing into my eyes, my ears, my nose, through every layer of clothing, wrapping itself like a coat of frost around my skin.

Unsure whether I was still pointed in the right direction, I kicked and groped at the water, trying to outswim the numbness, focusing on an earlier image of the opposite shore: an eddy of slack water curled behind a rock outcrop, and just below it was a small, sandy beach. I kicked harder, fighting the boils and whirlpools pulling me downstream.

When one of my arms hit slack water, I couldn't believe it. It was too quick, too early, but after two more strokes, my body slid across the shear of fast- and slow-moving water and came to rest in a deep eddy. I reached for the gray rock that rose above me, one hand closing on a nubbin of limestone, the other jamming into a crack, both hands too numb to feel the sharp edges rip and tear skin. My feet found an underwater ledge, and soon I was rising out of the water, shifting from swimming to climbing as the river streamed out of my clothes and ears, letting warmth and sound flood back in. Leanne whooped and hollered behind me, and when I turned to look around, I saw why:

I was upstream of the beach. I'd surfed.

With the rope still clenched in my fingers, I climbed to the canyon rim and set up my end of the high-line system while Leanne put the finishing touches on hers. Pulling it tight, we sent the packs across one by one, followed by the bags of food that had arrived in another airdrop the day before. Then, after we'd dismantled the system of knots and makeshift pulleys, Leanne gave me the thumbs up and strode in.

Before I could even grab my camera she was across, jet-ferrying the first half of the river, stroking and kicking like an Olympic swimmer for the second, coughing and sputtering as she pulled herself ashore. Clambering back down the cliff, I ran to meet her cold, heaving body as she staggered onto the beach.

"We're across the Firth!" I cried, hugging her hard. But we didn't celebrate for long, knowing the caribou easily could force us to do it all again.

Unlike the spring migration, during the summer movements of the caribou herd, there is no fixed destination, no postcalving grounds, no average migratory route we could default to if we didn't find the herd. Continuing to travel in the large, close-knit groups that banded up after calving, they roam widely and without pattern, moving in response to food, weather, predators, and, most of all, bugs. Some might head deep into the Yukon's mountains, others toward the east slopes of the Richardsons in the Northwest Territories, and, although we didn't like to admit it, some might circle back over the Firth, going so far as to return to the coastal plain. Following caribou had always been uncertain and indefinite, but now we were in the most unpredictable season of all.

Our time along the Firth had yielded nothing—no visions, dreams, caribou, or thrumming—and after a total wait of five days we'd found ourselves desperate for news. Putting the ideal of a land-based wisdom on the back burner, we pulled out the satellite phone and made the call, feeling like sellouts as we did.

The conversation with Dorothy was even shorter and more pointed than the one we'd made a month and a half before. Again, she fed us coordinates downloaded from the locations of seven radio-collared caribou, and again we plotted them on our worn map.

"These are too far, and they're heading away instead of toward us," Leanne said, pointing to the five that were scattered as far west as Alaska and as far east as the Babbage River. "But these," she stabbed her finger at the two closest ones, "these we might have a chance of finding."

I looked over her shoulder at the string of points that showed two animals hooking south into the mountains from the foothills, working their way up the Tuluqaq and Trail river valleys through the heart of Ivvavik National Park: if they stayed their course and slowed down, and if we swam the Firth River and hurried, our paths might cross in three or four days.

The Firth valley is an anomaly. Unlike other drainages on the North Slope, it contains trees. Not big ones, and not huge numbers of them, but trees nevertheless, peninsulas and islands of spruce and cottonwoods fingering up draws and spreading onto benches, some growing as tall as 20 feet.

It was nice to have those trees at first; not only did they provide shade from the ongoing hot, sunny weather but they also serve as markers denoting places where the soft, energy-sucking bogs that so typify these valley lowlands give way to strips of firm, dry ground. But all the advantages seemed to shift against us when we turned east up Wolf Creek: the previously scattered trees closed in around us, and what had been a parklike stroll became a thrash. Suddenly we were bushwhacking in the Arctic, pushing through thickets of prickly branches instead of lurching across tussocks, unsure which we hated more.

The bugs didn't help. No longer in the breeze that had kept them at bay along the Firth, we found ourselves digging deep to the bottom of our packs and donning nylon mesh head nets for the first time.

"I feel like I'm walking with a screen door pressed on my face," said Leanne, trying to shade the sun's glare on mesh with an out-stretched hand.

"You pretty much are," I said, also half-blind and stumbling. We stopped after a few minutes, lifted the nets long enough to wipe at the sweat streaming down our faces, then pulled them down again as clouds of mosquitoes swarmed from all sides. We resumed walking under the hot, stuffy, and claustrophobic head nets as a high whine filled the air around us, and we wondered how we were going to survive five to six weeks of such hell.

An old caribou trail wound through the dense, prickly forest, but the obstacle course of downed trunks and overhanging branches forced it to fork and split so many times that soon there was little path to follow at all. High-stepping, ducking, and even crawling at times, we pushed our way to what we thought was the end of a thicket, only to be stymied again.

"Well, it's not great, but it is better than tussocks," said Leanne once we'd covered a few miles.

I didn't agree. Although we were moving, there was none of the flow I associate with walking, none of the rhythm and relief that come after a prolonged sit. The loneliness and frustration that had descended over me while waiting along the Firth weren't going to disappear with a stroll into a new scene.

I attributed my hopelessness to the situation, but when we climbed out of the trees the next morning and I was still grumpy, Leanne labeled my inner turmoil for what it was.

"C'mon, Heuer, would you lighten up?" she demanded, pulling off my head net to show me the bug-free breeze. "What's with you? Don't tell me *you're* having your period now!"

It was as much a jab at herself as it was at me. Four days earlier, just as we'd started our vigil along the Firth River, I'd scarcely been able to talk to her without setting off an argument. Overnight, everything had become overwhelming—the trip, the filming, even tasks as simple as filling her water bottle in a nearby creek. But no sooner had the wave of despair and dread passed over her than it had engulfed me.

*July 7—Wolf Creek, Yukon—*Month Four, Week Thirteen, and our emotions grow more raw with each distraction-free day. There is no television to fill the gaps between high points, no idle chatter, background music, or advertisements to fill the day. This being alone with oneself is painful at times, agonizing with its hidden hormonal cycles, but it is also the most profound feeling in the world. When we are high, we are soaring; when we're low, we're rock-bottom; and the in-between times find us searching not just for caribou but for who we really are. Wildlife biologist turned dreamer and back again; a rational mind and a not-so-rational body discovering wildness for the first time. It's as though my spirit has split—cariboulike when I'm with the animals, humanlike when I'm not, crisscrossing the tundra in search of some middle ground.

Pink blooms of dwarf blueberry gave way to white stars of alpine heather as we climbed and crested the pass, and with the canyons, cliffs, and trees of the Firth River and Wolf Creek falling away behind us, we slipped into the wide basin of the Trail River.

"Well, this should make you happy," chuckled Leanne in reference to my earlier disdain for the forest. Jumbled ridges of loose, sharp rock fringed a huge, stadiumlike amphitheater, and from one side to the other stretched a gently rolling carpet of familiar-looking grass. My ankles ached just looking at it.

"Tussocks," Leanne mocked. "Not a tree in sight."

Wanting to be alone and in no mood for taunts, I pushed past her and continued on at a brisk walk, ensuring we traveled apart for most of the afternoon.

The smatterings of fresh scat and the occasional hoofprint that had first appeared near the top of Wolf Creek materialized again in the headwaters of the Trail River, but they were merely tiny points in a large world of possibilities, dots too hidden in the clefts of tussocks to be connected. After a few hours of trying, I gave up and stopped.

"Best to keep going," said Leanne as she brushed past. I shook my head and laughed, not sure whether I should love or hate a woman with such strength.

"Wait!" I called, struggling to catch up. "What are you following?"

Leanne hesitated, sighed, then started off again, mumbling something I didn't understand.

"Say again?"

"A feeling," she said, still not stopping as I struggled after her.

"A feeling? What kind of feeling?"

She spun and glared at me.

"Alright, Mr. Thrum. What were *you* following for the last three hours?"

I looked east, west, north, and south, then shrugged. Triumph flashed in Leanne's eyes.

"Well, then I guess a feeling is going to have to do."

I was still chafing at our squabbles when we stopped late that evening, still plagued by something I couldn't put my finger on and keen to pick a fight.

"You're not going to pull those off in here, are you?" I asked as Leanne began unlacing her boots inside the tent. She looked at the bugs popping off the outside walls, then back at me.

"Let me get this straight," she began. "You don't trust my route-finding, you can't stand my smells, you say my snoring and heavy breathing keep you awake ... so what is it about me that you love?"

It was a setup if I'd ever heard one, and for a split second I considered another cutting comment, but then something rose through the negativity and I saw what the hormones had shrouded for days: I looked at my wife and fellow adventurer, the one who hadn't complained once about spending more nights of our marriage on the ground than in a bed, the one who willingly had spent three and a half months moving from one set of parents' basement to the other after our wedding, all so we could embark on this crazy trip.

"Your spirit," I said, suddenly overcome with love. "Your smiling spirit."

I stood stunned beside the trampled trail. I'd never seen anything quite like it, not even during the postcalving rush: 2 feet wide and cutting right through the tussocks—every hummock and bulge in the otherwise lumpy tundra had been stamped perfectly flat.

"There must've been five or ten thousand," said Leanne.

"At least," I answered, too awestruck to say more. The patterns said everything—the black trench chiseled across the gold-green basin, a hundred lesser lines that spread and swirled into the grass before braiding back together and disappearing upward in a line of freshly fallen rocks. Traveling, feeding, stampeding; we could almost feel the wave of panic that had come when bugs had sent the herd clattering onto the ridge.

"We were right," said Leanne. "The Trail River. This is where we figured we might run into them. Only problem is, we're late."

I looked at the ridge, almost expecting to see the black silhouettes still up there, but all that stared down was the blistering sun.

At first I didn't mind that the animals weren't there; the marks of their passing were powerful enough. But as morning gave way to afternoon, afternoon to evening, and evening to three more days of looping, climbing, even backtracking along their trail, the excitement and energy began to wear off. After weeks of anticipation—after having leapt ahead and waited for an aggregation that never materialized along the Firth River—we wanted to actually see one of the big groups.

The trail took us through terrain that was nothing like what we'd seen on our way to the calving grounds earlier that spring. Meandering between 40 and 80 miles farther inland, we wound through the foothills south of the British Mountains instead of to their north and wove between cone-shaped hills and sharp, horseshoe-shaped ridges that wrapped around flat-bottomed basins on three sides. It was almost volcanic in character, as if the tectonic and erosional forces that had shaped the rest of the North Slope had failed to exert themselves in that corner, resulting in vast sweeps of knee-high cotton grass with rock ridges all around. It was the perfect place for hungry caribou bothered by bugs: good forage existed in the lowlands, and there were plenty of breezy refuges up high.

It was on those ridge tops or along their rocky margins that Leanne and I traveled, getting closer to the caribou the whole time. We had to be, for wherever the dark trails circled in the wide valleys and basins, we halved and quartered distances by going straight and by staying high where they climbed up and down. In such a way we gained valuable hours as we crossed the Trail valley, the headwaters of the Muskeg and Gravel drainages, and the ridge system that skirted Cottonwood Creek. By the time we reached the beginnings of the Babbage River and the eastern boundary of Ivvavik National Park, their trail was so fresh the spots of urine hadn't yet dried.

We saw our first animals early the next morning. Not the big group we were sure we were following, but scattered individuals that hobbled along the trail like ailing mountaineers.

"Stragglers," whispered Leanne, pointing to a trio of thin cows led by a calf and a limping bull.

"Like us," I said, watching as the calf waited every few steps for its slow-moving mother. Resolute and brave, they had no hint of defeat in their gait. Leanne and I each made a little bow as we passed them, then respectfully pushed on.

We encountered another cow-calf pair a mile later that didn't move at all. They're just feeding, drinking, and resting, I thought to myself as we began to skirt them, but then something odd made me stop.

"She's holding her head weird," I said to Leanne, pointing to where the cow stood bent and askew in a shallow creek. Her whole body was tilted and off balance, shaking and shuddering as her legs buckled and overcorrected, bending before suddenly jolting her upright as they snapped straight.

A small nose poked out from a nearby patch of willows, watching as the cow staggered and dropped its head onto a streamside pad of thick moss.

"The calf," Leanne pointed.

I nodded, then gestured back to the cow.

"She's dying."

Just as I said it, the cow lifted her head and a stream of thick, brown mucus oozed from her snout. Nose botflies were swarming her, discharging their larvae to join the legions that were already wreaking havoc deep inside her head. Attacking the respiratory system of their hosts, they are more bothersome than mosquitoes (which sometimes suck as much as a pint of blood from an animal in a week) and warble flies (whose larvae burrow through the caribous' hides and mature under their skin). As we were seeing, the wasplike, housefly-size bots were capable of the sort of harm one normally attributes to wolves.

When the cow coughed and sneezed and another glob of liquid streamed out, I grabbed Leanne's video camera and began to record. We were close—just 50 yards away—but the cow paid us no notice. Skull buzzing, she was deaf and blind, unaware that two people stood slightly above and behind her, one with his head behind a lens, the other just watching, both with tears in their eyes. Fighting for balance and relief, the cow swayed hard as she buried her snout back into the moss, then stumbled as her front legs gave out, sending her thin body slumping into the creek.

Watching her suffer was difficult, but it was the silence that impacted me the most: no moans, no groans, no cries or calls from the dying cow or her doomed calf. Just more of the extraordinary acceptance we'd already witnessed during the blizzard and wolves. Only the water had something to say; babbling as it had before the tormented cow arrived, as it would when she lay down for good.

I paused and looked back after we'd walked 100 yards. Despite my sadness, I smiled. The cow's head and body were quiet but her hooves were still moving, kneading the water that poured over them in an endless liquid trail.

Not a bloom of fireweed, seed of mountain avens, or part of any other plant had been left untrampled, and with the wild scent of caribou heavy in the air, Leanne and I strode past the flattened stems and leaves, anticipating what lay just ahead. It was a day later, and the trail we followed had only freshened with each mile since the dying cow. This time I was certain that when the slopes fell away and the view opened in another few minutes, we would witness the splendor of an aggregation beyond anything we'd imagined or dreamed. But when the hills did recede and a thousand-acre bowl of gently rolling tussocks spread before us an hour later, only the vastness of the Arctic stared back.

"I can't believe it," I said after scouring every square foot of the green, grassy expanse with binoculars. Leanne sat on her pack beside me, quietly watching as I threw my load beside hers and stormed off, searching for the trail that had suddenly disappeared. There were tracks, but they led everywhere—east, west, north, south—splitting and forking like thoughts coming apart. All the solid signs and trends we'd been following for the past four days had dissipated into a broth of conflicting hints. I looked again, searching, but the only movement was a pair of upland sandpipers, one singing on the tundra, the other stroking the sky with slow wing beats, keeping time with its mate's chattering tune.

"For Chrissakes!" I screamed.

The bird went quiet and a curtain of silence fell behind it, cutting off the comforting echo of my own confounded shout. I reached down and sifted a handful of rocks through my fingers, throwing off the strands of caribou hair that were left, then raged off again. I walked one direction and another, then in widening circles, swatting at mosquitoes and flies as the chaos of prints grew. Twenty minutes later I was more confused than ever. And then it hit me. I stretched my arms skyward, threw back my head, and laughed.

Our movements were being dictated by caribou whose movements were being dictated by bugs whose movements were being dictated by shifting winds.

I went back to where Leanne had started setting up the tent and shared my revelation. She laughed. We both laughed. We laughed at our stupidity, our idealism, our expectations, and then we laughed at how we looked: our greasy hair, our red eyes, our bug-bitten hands, our baggy, dirt-stained clothes and shiny, sunburned skin. Still chuckling, we dove into the tent, zipped the door shut, and, after killing every mosquito inside, dropped into a deep and carefree sleep.

> *July 14—Fish Hole Creek, Yukon—*After three months of feeling hammered, humiliated, tantalized, and disappointed, the weight lifts. We haven't given up on following caribou; we've given in. There is no angst this morning, no obsessive search that consumes the day. After three months of traveling, sleeping, and

eating with one focus, we let go of all expectations. In that moment, everything shifts.

Leanne and I walked side by side, following an unseen trail. There were no upturned rocks, no obvious tracks, no trampled plants, no reasons to stop and squint against the light. Heads clear and bodies singing, we followed signs we felt but couldn't see. It was as if we hadn't fully woken up that morning, and with our minds still foggy our feet had assumed the lead role in determining where we went next.

All that day, life was on the increase. The number of birds swelled as fledglings took to the air around us, Indian paintbrush and yellow ragweed bloomed by the creeks, and as we passed more injured and ailing caribou, a pair of goshawks swooped overhead, giving flight lessons to their young chicks.

And then we heard it: a rumbling that surged beneath our feet.

We ran more than walked toward it, winding our way to the end of the ridge to where a slope of half-buried boulders dropped away and disappeared beneath us in great plumes of evening mist. We were on the edge of something, some great expanse of space and life, and although part of us wanted to charge after it, something told us to sit and wait.

*July 16—Dog Creek, Yukon—*We are new at this, this following of intuition, and while pitching camp we second-guess whether it is right or wrong. After so long a time without being around caribou, it seems strange to stop walking now that we feel so close, and yet our hands and arms continue to set up the tent and cook dinner, not listening to our questioning minds. We climb into the tent out of the wind and, hunched over cups of soup, wonder why we sit instead of walk.

Grunts interrupted dinner. Abandoning our meal, we climbed out of the tent to investigate, matching foggy images to the huffs and coughs filtering through the rocks. Half a dozen caribou stood looking at our tent, with hundreds more filing behind them, carefully picking their way across the slick, lichen-covered boulders. Without a word, Leanne and I reached for cameras and lenses, our fingers fumbling with dials and buttons that hadn't been used for more than a week. I focused on one animal, only to have it move, then found another in the viewfinder, but it too pressed on. Finally I lowered the camera and just watched. One line of animals became two, and then the lines merged into a river many animals deep.

What happened in the next few moments was impossible to capture on film. While animals descended into the fog in front of us, holes opened in the cloud, offering a glimpse of the great gathering to which they were headed far below. I peered through one clearing and reached for binoculars, focusing on a dark blot of brown sliding across the greenness, but no sooner had I glimpsed it than another swirl of clouds closed in. I waited for another window in the cloud, looked into it, but was quickly thwarted again.

It took many openings for me to grasp the scale and scope of what I was witnessing, but as soon as I did, I called out to Leanne.

"There," I pointed, handing her the binoculars. Her eyes moved behind the lenses and then she gasped. Thrusting the glasses back at me, she reached for her camera and trained it down through the clouds, ignoring the animals still streaming all around.

Hundreds of feet below, and more than half a mile distant, the far-off patterns of movement commanded our attention now: huge fronts of life sweeping through a wide trough of tundra, blanketing it from side to side.

"They're like ants," Leanne said.

"Swarming."

"There must be six or seven thousand."

I agreed, trying to stitch together an overall picture from the snapshots of life that opened and closed in the clouds. Behind and to either side of us, clicking tendons reminded me of the hundreds more that still filed in.

"At least," I finally replied.

Bleary-eyed, Leanne hit the pause button half an hour later and looked up from the video camera. "Could this be it? Could this be the postcalving aggregation?"

I scanned around as the fog lifted, watching as other lines descended off other slopes, gathering into a knot of thousands of animals below. It wasn't quite the stampeding chaos and churning dust I'd imagined it would be, but it was spectacular. Dozens of streams of caribou converged into a sweep of bodies and antlers, spreading and contracting as it moved, inhaling and exhaling up the hillsides and into the hollows, expanding and shrinking as it floated along the valley in long, easy breaths.

"Pretty sure," I nodded.

Leanne looked pleased as she settled in beside me. It had taken months of effort to get here, weeks of frustration, and in the end it wasn't satellite collars, scientific reports, maps, or even tracks that had guided us in. It was the thrumming. Even now, sitting on the rocky slope as the caribou amassed a thousand feet below, we could feel it—a potential that throbbed all around: in the animals pouring past our camp, in the throng of life below us, in the rocks, flowers, birds, even the tussocks, rising in goose bumps that crawled over our skin.

Thick clouds sent us to bed; bright sun got us up. Leanne crawled out of the tent first, and the ensuing long silence negated my need to ask. What had been full of caribou a few hours earlier was empty once again. But this time there was no need to worry. Underneath the silence rolled the deep, comforting sound.

"Somewhere over . . . there," I guessed, waving east and around the corner. Leanne listened for a moment, cocking her head from side to side, then concurred.

We didn't travel far—a few hundred yards in that direction—before they came into view, a tightly packed ball of animals contracting and expanding farther east in the same wide valley, spinning in one direction and then the other in a strange, incomprehensible dance. We watched for a long time from our high vantage, long enough for a dying breeze to send every one of them running to the top of the closest ridge, turning its gray summit brown with their bodies as they farmed the heights for wind. When the breeze did pick up, they poured back down and immediately fed.

I turned to Leanne, gesturing in the direction of the wind. "It's at our back. They're going to drift this way."

She nodded and we quickly descended from our lookout into the valley, hunching hands deep into our sleeves and cinching head nets tight around our necks. With no place to hide ourselves, we lay down on the tundra, leaning on our packs.

The front of thousands of caribou neared, 400 yards, 300 yards, then a swarm of mosquitoes hit and the animals ran back before regrouping, then moved our way again.

We did our best to sit quietly, but the bugs were intense. Not a sliver of our accessible skin went unnoticed, and we fidgeted, trying to loosen clothing around knees, elbows, and wherever else a stinger got in. It was all supposedly bug-proof, but these were no ordinary bugs. With only a month to feed, breed, and reproduce, they were voracious beyond imagining, not particular about whether it was humans or caribou they attacked so long as it was fresh blood. We swatted and swiped just enough to survive, waiting as the harassed animals slowly neared.

After a few painful minutes, our self-discipline paid off. The wind picked up, and all the back-and-forth charging gave way to a solid advance. With the lead animals only 100 yards off, we would soon be engulfed.

Having seen the dying cow four days earlier, Leanne and I knew the mass of caribou would be distracted by bugs, but neither of us predicted to what extent. As they approached, there was no hint of their old behavior—none of the skittishness of the calving grounds, none of the vigilance or attentive looks; no maintaining the 100-yard distance they'd always kept between us during the spring migration. Though we were lying there in plain view on the tussocks, the animals closed in as though we didn't exist. Fifty yards, 30 yards, 20 yards … Leanne and I exchanged worried looks as the lead cows and bulls continued their approach, stamping, snorting, and coughing in raspy breaths. When contact seemed inevitable, when it seemed we were going to be stepped on, I softly spoke out.

"Hey."

A line of six animals paused three paces away while hundreds of others drifted like a moving canvas behind them, half-chewed flowers and blades of grass dangling from their lips. There was no panic, no alarm stance, none of the usual pissing or pawing when we happened too close. This time they simply looked up for a few suspended seconds, then proceeded as before, continuing to feed.

Within minutes we were surrounded. Grunting bulls grazed alongside coughing cows, encircling us in a forest of legs. Through it came a pair of calves, one approaching within arm's length before tentatively stepping back, the other not even looking as it settled down just beyond my feet and promptly fell asleep. I watched the heap of fur rise and fall while legions of animals drifted behind it, marveling at how, within the span of a half hour, we were in the midst of what we'd observed from above, two points of color in a dark wheel of animals that shifted and spun in the wind.

Even with a brisk breeze to keep the insects away, the harassment we witnessed was surprising. Not a second passed without an animal shuddering, not a minute without an outbreak of fly-induced snorts and sneezes. Feet stamped, hooves scratched against the mosquitoes, and through all the unrest charged the odd wild-eyed animal, bucking and kicking in its itchy skin. The calves, too, were bothered. There was no playing, none of the frolicking of the calving grounds. The air of joyful innocence had been whittled away by the miles and bugs, and what remained was the hard edge of existence where there was no spare energy, just time to eat, move, and, if the wind allowed it, sleep. The calf at my feet came awake and flicked its hind leg, kicking until a persistent fly flew off.

The changes in the caribou were physical as well as behavioral. Up close, the animals looked harried, especially the cows, whose bleached winter fur hung in clumps from summer coats that hadn't yet grow in. Even the perfect fur of the calves was blemished and pockmarked with scars and bites. Only the bulls, cloaked in sleek summer coats, looked healthy, but they too had undergone change. There was less velvet on their antlers, less fat on their stomachs. After only two weeks, the bugs had taken their toll on every body, but more on the caribou than on us. My complaints seemed trivial in comparison. They had no bug nets or bug-proof clothing, no screened tent for a much-needed respite. Their sole defense against the bugs was the same as it had been against the wolves, bears, blizzards, and every other challenge we'd seen them face: keep moving, no matter the cost.

There were costs late that afternoon when the wind died. Just as we'd interpreted from the circling tracks and back-and-forth trails of the previous week, the animals that contentedly fed one moment were in a panic the next, running every which way as clouds of mosquitoes set in and chaos broke out in the herd. We didn't stay still in those moments, moving just enough not to get trampled, disoriented by the effort of trying to track animals that raced all around us. Calves bleated in the pandemonium, cows huffed, and then they all headed for the ridge, led by a contingent of bulls.

"Oh no, not this again," Leanne cried as churning hooves worked a treadmill of loose rocks down on the last few straggling calves. Some followed despite the hazard, but others spooked and turned back toward us.

"Find your mother," I growled, jumping up and flapping my arms, but it was no use. Eyes blinking and bodies twitching, two of the six calves just stood there while the other four kept running, descending into the heart of the buggy basin instead of climbing into the wind. A few cows came clambering down the rocks and set off after them, but within minutes a wave of flies and mosquitoes turned them back as the youngsters raced off. Leanne and I watched the calves grow smaller until they were nothing but four brown specks streaking across the vast, green tundra, splitting, arcing, and spinning toward oblivion, until the tussocks seemed to swallow them whole.

By noon we were dizzy with heat, sweltering in black pants, long-sleeve shirts, and bug nets, craving shade where none existed. There was no breeze, no relief from the stifling heat or insects, and we lay on our packs watching the caribou stand motionless on the broad, rocky ridge 1,000 feet above. Sweat trickled down our backs as heat shimmers rose off the rocks, twisting and distorting the tormented animals into grotesque and ghostly shapes.

"Should we go up?" I asked two hours later. Among the thousands of caribou lined shoulder to shoulder along the ridge for more than a mile, not one had moved.

Leanne nodded, pulling her hands from her sleeves to swipe at the hovering cloud above her. "Anything to get out of these bugs."

July 19—Dog Creek Ridge, Yukon—Time stands still.
For two days we sit watching the caribou, and for

two days they stand, heads hung low, mouths agape,
watching us. It is hard to see them like this, robbed
of their mobility and starving in the rocks like statues
of their former selves. But even in their stillness they
guide us, showing patience where Leanne's and mine
have worn thin, faithfully waiting for a bug-free wind.

The tent fluttered, and through the whine and buzz of insects
came the sound of hooves.

"Typical males," remarked Leanne as she looked out. While the
bulls stood and watched, a contingent of half a dozen cows and
calves picked their way down through the piles of loose rock. It
was a vicious pattern of diminishing returns we'd seen a few times
before. Still lactating and still trying to gain back weight lost on the
spring migration, the cows—the animals that could least afford the
energy—were the ones most driven by hunger to descend and feed.
They usually didn't last more than a few mouthfuls before the bugs
inevitably turned them back, but this time it was different. After
descending the precarious slope, the cow-calf pairs stepped onto the
tussocks, fed solidly for five minutes, then spread out.

A murmur passed through the herd watching from the ridge.

"They're going," I chimed in, already stuffing the sleeping bag into
my pack. As if on a signal, the stagnant mass of animals was shifting
into motion. Hundreds of calves quietly searched out their mothers,
outliers from the herd gradually moved in, and then the throng of
thousands turned and began to descend from the site of their two-day
vigil, filling the air with a guttural hum.

The wind didn't quit blowing once it started, and for the next
three days we fell into a stop-and-go rhythm that was almost effortless.
Caressed by the breeze, we had no need for head nets, no long waits
in the stifling heat, no charges up and down the slopes trying to keep
up with caribou keeping out of bugs. Waiting on the margins of the

basins as the animals ventured to feed out in the middle, Leanne and I wrote, ate, and even read, sitting on makeshift tussock-couches and boulder-stools. Sometimes it was a few minutes before the caribou wandered on and we followed them, sometimes many hours, but it was never far to the next rest stop, going first one way and then another, crisscrossing over low, horseshoe-shaped ridges on trails that were neither too shallow nor too steep.

"There's no pattern," I said to Leanne after I'd plotted the three days of looping, meandering travel on the map. There didn't need to be. Winter was still a month or two ahead, and for the time being, there were no wolves, bears, or bugs. The caribou were simply drifting and feeding for the first time all trip.

"No pattern," Leanne agreed, "but why are you smiling?"

I looked up, still grinning as I pointed to the freshly drawn line on the map. It tracked straight for the first dozen or so miles east of the British Mountains, then wavered, veering south before it hit the Barn Range and looped west back on itself. Leanne saw straight away the joke it spelled.

"We've moved in a giant question mark!"

The next day the wind dropped and the caribou gravitated back toward the ridge where Leanne and I waited, then they swung south along an alleyway of mostly buried boulders that skirted its base. Fringed by ankle-breaking tussocks on one side and leg-snapping talus on the other, the strip of firm and relatively smooth ground made for good traveling, and we managed to keep pace as we followed a few hundred yards behind.

"Not bad," I said after we'd been going five hours without breaking a sweat.

No answer.

"It's good, isn't it?"

Still nothing.

"Leanne?"

And that's when I realized the creature breathing behind me wasn't my wife.

When a pair of hooves stepped into view, I kept looking forward, my whole upper body going rigid with shock. "Keep walking," I said to myself, and I did, not missing a beat in the hope that the rhythm that had taken me to the edge of this moment would carry me in. Antlers took shape, then legs, snout, chest, and the rest of the body. Still I walked and still the bull pulled alongside me, its head and neck bobbing in time with my stride while two more big males edged in.

Had I taken two steps sideways, I could have reached out and touched them, but there was no need: I could hear, smell, and feel them as their nostrils whooshed, bodies sweated, and brown eyes rolled up and down, inspecting me as I, in turn, inspected them. The cracked and splitting hooves; the scarred forelegs; the mounds of rippling muscle that rose off their dark brown rumps and shoulders, contrasting with the thick, white ruff of their heaving chests.

My body held marks from the migration as well—scratched shins, scabbed knees, hollowed-out spaces between my ribs—but they were hidden beneath nylon clothing, which, after so many miles and months, was the only layer I had left. Everything else had been shed—my false sense of security, my hubris, my mental clutter—and what it allowed me to do in that moment was simply relax. The bulls seemed to sense this: their eyes softened, their breathing quieted, and for a brief, suspended moment we moved in unison, heartbeats and footsteps mingling while we inhaled each other's exhaled breaths. Finally, after so many miles, I was floating with animals instead of chasing them. I was experiencing caribou experiencing themselves.

There were four more animals that came once the bulls pulled ahead—a pair of cows with their calves—and they too behaved as though I were invisible, passing a few yards away before moving on.

Finally, a shallower, more familiar pattern of breathing sounded from behind. I turned as a pair of hiking boots came into view.

"I feel like a kid again," said Leanne as she pulled up beside me. Her eyes were as clear as I'd ever seen them, and the lines of worry that had knit her brow for the last three and a half months were gone. I reached out and squeezed her hand. Those six words summarized exactly how I was feeling. We had broken free of the textbook mentality that separated the world into needs, wants, and resources and had returned to a younger, sweeter version of what was possible in life.

A day and a half later we found ourselves at the top of the last in a long line of U-shaped ridges and lush basins where the caribou had circulated for much of the previous week. The beginnings of the much higher Barn Range lay just ahead to the east, the last of the British Mountains were behind us, and for the first time since the spring, we caught glimpses of Old Crow Flats creeping out from the dark band of tree line far to the south.

It was over that distant, spaghettilike arrangement of winding creeks and glittering lakes that storm clouds brewed later that afternoon, billowing and mushrooming skyward until the breeze marched them into the caribou-filled basins where we walked. There, with no one but us watching, animals, thunder, and lightning crashed together in bolts of energy and life.

There was no running for cover in that moment—no cover, period—and while we got soaked, the caribou ran headlong into the storm, letting it pull every extra hair, bug, and seed from their coats in a hammer of swirling gusts and rain. Not bothering to pull on our anoraks or Gore-Tex pants, we let the same storms wash over our own bodies, rinsing away the dirt, sweat, and itchy bug bites, bringing a welcome chill to the run-on sunny nights and heat-filled days. But no sooner had the storm started than it was over. The sun found a hole in the shrinking clouds, the swirling gusts gave way to a steady, stiff breeze, and we stripped off our wet clothes, tied them to our packs, and walked in underwear until everything was dried.

"Hey, whitey!" Leanne called after me.

I stopped and turned to look at my wild-haired wife walking in bra and panties, her limbs no less pale than mine. The tan lines were sharp: hands, face, and neck darkened by three and a half months of outdoor living, offset by arms and torso that hadn't seen sunlight in more than 100 days. But with the nearest town more than 200 miles away, it didn't matter what either of us looked like. We traipsed across the tundra half-naked, following caribou that neither noticed nor cared.

"The caribou knew this was coming."

"Knew what was coming?"

"This weather," Leanne barked over the north wind. "They knew it was going to change."

I fiddled with the tent's guy lines and tie-downs as another wave of wet snow slapped my face.

"Think about it," she continued, pulling off her wet clothes and hurrying into the sleeping bag once we were inside. "It's why they've been splitting into smaller and smaller groups. They knew this snow-storm was on its way."

I thought about the last two days, how the group that had done nothing but grow since the calving grounds had suddenly started to split and dissipate for no apparent reason. And then I thought about the story we'd heard in Old Crow before leaving, the one in which the caribou had turned partway through their fall migration and headed north instead of south, perplexing not only the hunters but every biologist that had ever studied the herd. Only when a freak midwinter ice storm hit three months later and coated their usual winter range with a thick layer of ice had their actions made sense. We were following not only supreme travelers but psychics as well.

The storm caught us off guard both mentally and physically. After three weeks of hot weather, we'd thought we were done with such sudden shifts of season, and yet here we were, freezing at noon in the same tent we'd sweltered in the night before. Using hands that were bug-bitten and red with sunburn, I reached into the vestibule to light the stove, but my fingers were too numb. Fumbling once then twice, I picked up the lighter and tried again.

"So much for a friendly, bug-free wind," muttered Leanne as another gust hit. Ten seconds later, every tent peg pulled loose and she bolted outside while I dove on the bucking floor.

For the rest of the afternoon, we worked to keep the tent upright, piling rocks on ropes and pegs only to take them off again when the wind veered and threatened us with a pole-breaking gust. When that happened, we went outside and reset everything, returning a little bluer in the face and our clothes covered in white. Snow followed freezing rain and ice fog, a building pattern of moisture and cold that repeated itself in four-hour waves. There were a few lulls, even some distant blue patches of sky, but each time one approached, the wind circled and mounded the fog back over us, reinventing the storm that had just passed.

After forty-eight hours, we emerged sleepless and blinking into what seemed a nice day. But no sooner had we scraped and stripped the tent of ice than the air grew heavy.

I shook my head. "Rain."

Leanne pulled up her hood and glowered at the sky. "No kidding."

"So what do you want to do?"

She shrugged her shoulders, but in the time it took her to do so, the decision was made. "We're already wet," she said. "We might as well walk and get warm."

There was something unsteady about the way we left, and it worsened with each passing hour. We were tired, hungry, soaked, and cold, to be sure, but it was more than that. After ten intense days with thousands of caribou, walking without them didn't seem right. We passed a few stationary individuals that fed, stood, or slept in the bugless rain and, after another hour of seeing no others, took it as a sign to camp. But in the time we'd walked, the snow that had blanketed the ground was now water, and what started as a hasty search for a dry campsite turned into a miles-long hunt. Even the high gravel banks of the Blow River were flooded, and we waded into its muddy current hopeful of finding something drier on the other side.

I was so cold the water felt warm when I stepped in, and I stopped, fighting off a wave of dizziness as it wrapped around my thighs. But while I steadied myself, Leanne pushed past, climbed ashore, and, without so much as a glance back, marched off in her distinctive we-need-to-stop-soon gait. With the first shivers taking hold, I picked up my pace and stumbled after her, tripping through the standing water and driving rain.

When we finally found 10 square feet of water-free ground, the rain had turned to snow again, soaking our bodies with a thick layer of heat-sapping slush. We unrolled the already wet tent, and while I fumbled with straps and buckles, Leanne swung her arms and told me to hurry, slurring her words. Somehow the tent got up and the sleeping bag came out, but nothing more. We forgot about the open packs and scattered gear on the whitening tundra and, after fiddling with wet lighters and depleted fuel bottles, forewent hot drinks and food. Still wearing wet clothes, we climbed into the bag and huddled together, waiting for warmth that never came.

> *July 26—Headwaters of the Blow River, Yukon—*We are gripped all night by shivers and hunger, and I wake in the morning grasping at arms, legs, and torso too thin to be my own. The fat was gone weeks ago, and now it is muscle that's being burned, slowly giving way to bone. I can't help but think of the irony. With

the arrival of cool weather and the worst of the bugs
past, the caribou will just be reaching their prime—as
I waste away. Being caribou and being human: today
there don't seem to be any similarities at all.

Leanne cooked breakfast while I searched for boots, camera cases, and clothing underneath the 4-inch snowfall, giving each item a shake before laying it on a rock to dry in the sun. The day held promise—only a few cigar-shaped clouds hung over the handful of grazing caribou that dotted the valley—but it wasn't promising enough to ease the scare of the night before. Even sitting there in the sun while the snow melted around us, we shivered, unable to generate heat.

"We cut it close last night," Leanne began, rubbing at the goose bumps on her skin. "I'm worried about these next few weeks. We don't have any reserves. If a river crossing, a bear encounter . . . if anything goes wrong . . ."

I nodded as her voice trailed off. I knew what she was driving at, and as much as I hated to admit it, I couldn't disagree. I reached into my pack for the maps.

Feeling as though I was betraying everything the caribou had taught us, I spent the next hour measuring distances, discussing dates, and plotting the few places that a plane could land between the village of Old Crow and where we sat. My lips uttered the mileages and my voice cited the dates and coordinates, but it wasn't me who made the plan.

It was someone I'd once been.

Someone I'd since forgotten.

Someone I didn't want to become again.

fall migration

I live my life in widening circles
that reach out across the world.
I may not complete this last one
but I give myself to it.

—Rainer Maria Rilke, *The Book of Hours*

We were just at the beginning of our apprenticeship with caribou—about dreaming, about thrumming, about listening with our whole bodies—yet that apprenticeship had come to a sudden end. We would head for Bonnet Lake for our second-to-last food drop, we decided, and from there walk directly south to Summit Lake. There, deep in the Richardson Mountains, we would receive our last supply of food, along with a borrowed canoe, and paddle down the Bell and Porcupine rivers. If all went according to plan and the weather cooperated, we would be back in Old Crow in three or four weeks.

Within hours of embarking, however, a grizzly bear ambled toward us, tracking west across the Blow River valley while we ventured east. Being weak, susceptible, and now focused on the future, our acceptance of everything unknown, unsafe, and unpredictable now slipped away.

"We don't need this now," I said, fingering the canister of bear spray holstered to my hip. But at 300 yards away, we remained unnoticed. Tacking left then right, a little up then a little down, the bear contoured around a small hill, digging as it went, stopping every once in a while to pounce. We waited while it passed and, when we were sure it wasn't returning, climbed to the same path and wrapped around the slope in the opposite direction.

"Hey, check this out!" Leanne nudged her boot at a spot of blood. Beside it was the freshly cleaved head of a ground squirrel, a look of surprise frozen on its face. Another few steps yielded another bodiless victim, followed by a third.

"The grizzly version of energy bars!" Leanne announced. "Which reminds me," she patted her pocket, "is it time yet?"

I glanced at my watch. With few caribou around and no longer any reason to observe or follow them, our minds were suddenly consumed by food and time. Partitioning the few supplies we had left, we figured exactly how much we could eat and when. I gulped down the bite-size piece she handed me.

"That's it?"

"That's it," mumbled Leanne, still savoring hers. Low on food, we were again on half rations, nibbling instead of snacking, snacking instead of having meals.

"Before long, it'll be us eating the ground squirrels," I joked.

She swallowed and laughed. "That'll be the day."

By the time we were ready to go again, the grizzly had disappeared, melting into the tussocks that stretched right back to the Barn Range, lost in the waves and dips of tundra that seemed smooth and featureless from afar. I scanned everything while looking for it—the cleft of every small creek that fed into the Blow River, the fields of rock that spilled off the hills and onto tundra—then stopped. Something else moved across the oceanlike surface, something darker than the blond grizzly and farther back.

"Look!" I pointed beyond our last camp, beyond the river, and across the glistening tussocks to where we'd waited out the storm two days before. The air was cool and clear, and through it we saw dots in the distance. It was just a few caribou at first, but soon there were hundreds trickling out of the mountains, pooling in the green trench of the Blow valley then drifting toward us like a slow-moving cloud. We watched for a half hour, long enough to see two other groups take form—one from the north, another from the west—both veering our way.

"They're coming to pick us up!" Leanne crowed.

I smiled. What she said sounded silly, but we were both ready to believe it. Widely dispersed for the last few days, they were suddenly banding together and bolting in our direction, and for what? There were no bugs to speak of, no wolves loping over the horizon. It was as if they weren't done telling us their stories and, with the news of our departure, were coming to lure us back into being caribou.

"Well?" Leanne asked two hours later.

I was still too shocked to talk. Among the many animals that had passed were the biggest bulls yet, charging across a creek so close to me that I was doused with spray from their hooves.

"Well?" she repeated. "Do we follow or do we stick to our plan?"

Torn between what my heart wanted and what my head said was right, I pulled out the compass and trained it on the place where the animals had just disappeared.

"Due south," I grinned. There was no need to part company. We were all heading toward Bonnet Lake.

> *July 25—Blow River, Yukon*—There have been too many coincidences over the last four months, too many signs appearing at just the right moment, to attribute everything to luck. There are so many places in this vast assemblage of mountains, valleys, and coastal plain where there aren't any caribou, yet day after day we stumble onto them, or them onto us. They seem

to wait when we've fallen behind, stop, even circle when we're delayed by weather, always appearing to guide us as though there's something they don't want us to miss.

For two days the caribou took us over familiar ground: up the hills we'd skied down almost four months earlier, down the slopes we had slogged up. We passed the site where we'd dried everything after the blizzard, revisited old lunch spots, even photographed and filmed caribou from behind the same boulder we'd used the spring before. The ground was green now instead of white; the arnicas, fleabane, and other flowers that had been buried in snow had bloomed and gone to seed; and the caribou now moved in the reverse direction—but the landmarks were the same. Climbing to the top of a knoll that rose above the others, we pulled out the binoculars and shouted out names we'd given each place four months before.

"The Place Where Many Creatures Have Seen Many Things," Leanne shouted, pointing to the beginnings of the Driftwood River to the southeast. I studied the two rock towers where we'd sat with a pair of goshawks as the direction of the spring migration had changed before us, then I glassed the creek bottom where we'd surprised the wolves.

"No predators today."

"No, but a few caribou under Misty Ridge." Leanne paused then laughed. "Three months later, and the top is *still* in fog."

For a half hour we rolled through names that meant nothing to anyone else—Willow Flats, Wolf Hill—then sat back on our haunches to watch caribou filter through all of it.

"They're spreading out again," said Leanne.

Indeed, the big groups that had briefly formed were dispersing, and with them we felt the surge of energy they'd brought wind down.

"They could go anywhere," I added, reciting what I'd read in the report about the fall migration. It was really more a slow, individual drifting than a typical migration. Once the bugs died, there was little reason for the animals to stay gathered, and they moved to wherever there was food, in pairs, trios, maybe a dozen, but no big groups.

We sat in silence imagining the possibilities: back to Alaska; out to the Arctic coast; down to Old Crow Flats and the Porcupine River. Soon there would be a new net of wandering, circling lines spreading out before us, and strung across each of them would be caribou, like notes in a song.

We had walked those lines, we had heard the singing, and we swore to ourselves, no matter what happened we would never forget.

The old exploration camp at Bonnet Lake was even uglier without the blanket of snow that had cloaked it in May. Rusting gas cans and old blasting wires littered the beach, and leading away from each of the three plywood shacks was a trail of dented and twisted metal. Although the snowdrifts that had choked them earlier were now gone, the buildings still offered little in the way of shelter. Entire walls had been pried away by bears and storms, and what was left of the floors, tables, and shelving was covered with piles of rodent droppings inches deep. Assuming we wouldn't be staying long, we pitched the tent on a patch of nearby ground.

If the jaeger that circled above us was any indication, it was perfect weather for flying. Spreading its small wings wide, it soared like an eagle in the updrafts of wind and sun. Stomachs growling, we pulled out the satellite phone and made the call to Inuvik, adding an extra order of butter, french fries, and pizza to the food drop already waiting to be flown in. Assured by the pilot that he would arrive in a couple of hours, we broke open the emergency pack of store-bought freeze-dried pasta I'd been carrying since Kaktovik.

"Tastes like soaked cardboard," Leanne complained after I'd boiled it up.

"Who cares what it tastes like," I said. "It's food."

"Hardly," Leanne retorted. "What's the expiration date?"

"May 2000," I said sheepishly. "But it was free."

She reluctantly swallowed another few spoonfuls while I cast aside the package and recalled the strange path it had taken to get here.

"This was made in California," I began, "shipped to a store in Vancouver, mail-ordered to Inuvik, flown to Aulavik National Park on Banks Island before Parks Canada donated it to us, flown back to Inuvik, driven to Calgary where we packed it last winter, trucked up to the Yukon last spring, mailed to Kaktovik, flown into the refuge by Walt in late June, then carried here by me!" I lay back, breathless and laughing.

"Well, then I guess I better eat it," chuckled Leanne.

"I guess so!"

When the plane still hadn't arrived by late evening, good humor turned to worry. In the distance the clouds were building, and when the wind died we scurried around the dilapidated buildings gathering every piece of rusted iron and heavy wood to better anchor the tent pegs. We knew what was coming. After a lull of only a few minutes, the breeze came back on itself, bringing fog, snow, and the beginnings of another tent-shaking storm.

For four days we waited—four days without any food—watching the sky, hoping for something different. There were sunny breaks, but they were fleeting, and we rushed into them picking blueberries, returning colder and wetter than we'd left.

"Is it any use?" I asked Leanne.

"What else are we going to do?"

I shrugged and watched as a pair of caribou bulls drifted along the misty shoreline not far from the tent. Scattered groups of up to a dozen animals had drifted in and out of view since we'd been waiting, there one minute, gone the next, never gone long before others took their place.

"People in Old Crow are going to laugh pretty hard if we starve surrounded by caribou," I said.

It was meant as a joke, but the word "starve" hung in the air long after I'd uttered it. This wasn't like the Aichilik or any of the other times we'd had to wait a day or two. With our physical reserves at an all-time low and the weather growing cooler, the situation was among the most serious we'd faced yet.

> *August 8—Bonnet Lake, Yukon*—I am dizzy and light-headed, fumbling through simple tasks. In the morning I spill half our precious stove fuel; in the afternoon, lose our fishing line in a botched cast into the lake. Weak and shaky, I give up on the evening berry-picking, fall into the tundra, and wait for some unseen wisdom to come. But all that arrives are three feeding caribou. As they venture to within a dozen yards, it's impossible for me not to notice how much their condition has improved. Even the two cows have put on weight, their dark, silky summer coats pulled tight over bodies that actually show some fat for the first time all trip.

Every time the clouds lifted, we spotted an almost perfectly white grizzly bear across the half-mile-wide lake, and after five days of watching it graze berries, I took its sudden switch to digging for ground squirrels as a cue. Armed with a length of snaring wire and a few willow stakes, I searched out holes on our side of the lake while the bear dug up those on his. Three hours and many adjustments later, I was back at the tent, a successful hunter returning to his mate.

"You expect me to eat that?" Leanne asked, looking at the muddy corpse hanging from my hand. "It looks like a drowned rat."

Her comment did little to stop my drooling.

"You can keep picking berries if you want," I replied, "but this is meat."

Unconvinced, she stood aside as I gutted and skinned it, cringing as I chopped and dropped the pieces into the pot.

The smell of it cooking finally won her over. After watching me take a few satisfied bites, she tentatively joined in.

"Those bears are onto something," she said after wolfing down half.

I nodded, still sucking at greasy bones. We weren't full, but we were happy. Unlike the thousands of berries we'd consumed, the protein and fat spread from our bellies in a wave of warmth.

"More?"

Leanne nodded, laughing as I set off to stake a fresh set of holes.

There was no action on the trapline until late the next morning, but this time the tripped snare held a squirrel that was alive, not dead. I dug it out from where it held fast in its hole, then brought a rock down on its head. It wasn't pretty, but after a few fumbled strikes the mangled mass of burst blood vessels and dislocated eyes finally went limp. Cutting away the worst of it, I stumbled back to camp feeling sick.

I don't know whether I'd have had the stomach to eat that one, but fortunately there was no need. Over the roar of the cookstove came another sound. I turned to shout to Leanne, but she was already on the beach fiddling with video camera and tripod. After six hungry days, two weeks' worth of food and fuel were finally coming in.

After one low pass, the floatplane banked and touched down on the water, taxiing to where we stood waving on the shore. Wading into the water, I grabbed a wing as the floats nudged the gravel, nodding to the pilot that I would hold it from running aground. Without so much as a wave, he hopped onto one of the floats and began unloading.

"How's it going?" I called over the wind.

"Good, good," he replied without looking up. "Listen, I can't stay and chat. Too much to do."

Not having seen or talked to anyone but Leanne for weeks, I wondered if I'd heard right. "Pardon me?"

Edgy and nervous, the young pilot eyed the weather and his wristwatch as he tossed our boxes ashore. "I'm in a hurry," he barked.

Another voice called from the plane. "Excuse me ..." A young woman, probably the pilot's girlfriend, leaned out the passenger window with her point-and-shoot camera.

"Do you mind if I take your picture?" she asked.

"Say again?"

"Your picture. Can I take it?" Not waiting for an answer, she took the photo. "Are you guys doing some kind of research out here?" she asked, wrinkling her nose as she stepped onto the float and pulled on a sweater. Its brightness, along with everything else she wore, assaulted my senses. It was all so clean, so white, so out of place against the muddy browns and gritty greens of the shoreline, not to mention our own filthy, sweaty clothes.

"Like I said, we gotta keep moving," interrupted the pilot after handing me the last box. Then in a push off the shore and a turn of the engine they were gone, zooming over the lake into the clouds, carrying snapshots of people and places they hadn't really met.

"Damn! I forgot to ask whether they saw many caribou."

Leanne rested her hand on my shoulder. "Don't worry, Karst. A guy like that wouldn't notice them unless they were lying on his runway."

*August 9—Bonnet Lake, Yukon—*These planes dropping out of the sky and into our lives are like a hiccup in time, but for all their disturbance they are a gift as well.

Not only do they bring food but they offer a glimpse into what we left months ago and what we'll return to in another few weeks: A world of hurried schedules and deadlines. A world where people rush from point to point without a sense of the land, animals, and plants between. A world long on money but short on thought. Tonight, still shocked by the behavior of the pilot, Leanne and I make a commitment to one another: no matter what happens when we return, no matter how difficult and painful it is to be back "home," we will try to live with the awareness and mindfulness we have now.

Friends in Inuvik had packed plenty of treats in the food boxes, and we would have stayed and gorged ourselves for days if it weren't for the white bear. Having exhausted the supply of berries and squirrels on its shore, it moved toward ours, closing to within 300 yards as we gulped down a homemade pizza, a box of fresh cookies, and two beers. The bear stayed occupied for the moment, but we knew it was only a matter of time before the vein of berries it was harvesting ran out. When it did, we didn't want to be around.

Leaving Bonnet Lake was like walking into a different season. Bloody-hued clumps of bearberry splashed across the tundra, and down every hillside streamed lines of willow and birch bushes like yellow and orange scarves. The green chord that had strummed all summer now struck different notes of vibrant color, and we walked among all of them, stirring the scent of curing heather and Labrador tea with each step.

Even the birds changed. Ptarmigan chicks lifted before us in silhouettes that were bigger than I remembered, and the waterfowl that had been bright and colorful all summer now wore their drab winter plumage. Long-tailed ducks, wigeons, and scoters collected on the ponds in gray shapes, and above us flew the cutout images of geese and swans in brown and white Vs. In less than a week the land had shifted around us, turning its back on summer and its sights on fall.

Winding along the hard banks of the upper Driftwood River, we backtracked our old ski route for the next two days. The abundance of life that had existed in that wide valley during the intense spring migration was diminished, but it was more diverse. The pair of goshawks still soared overhead, along with a recent fledgling; a myriad of sandpipers and songbirds flitted through the tundra; and through it all wandered first a grizzly and then a wolf. Neither chased the few caribou that watched with passing interest, nor did the predators acknowledge us. It was as though a truce had been proclaimed and all the fear and tension that had existed in that valley four months earlier had disappeared. There were no sudden movements, no radical shifts in direction or pace, no bugs or other predators preparing to ambush or stalk caribou or us. Even the weather had grown benign. With both the Barn and the northern Richardson mountains rising like a wall behind us, the fog and cold winds of the Arctic Ocean were held at bay. The nights were growing cooler, and we were peppered by the occasional rain and snow shower, but the majority of days were full of warm sun.

Aside from our weakening condition, our chief concern became the rivers. Frozen and easily crossed in the spring, they were now formidable barriers that pushed us deeper and higher into the Richardson Mountains, right up to the Arctic-Pacific Divide. The land was more rugged here than where we'd skied in the spring—craggy peaks and cliffs forced us off the ridge tops—but in the intervening passes and high valleys we found what we needed: knee-deep fords instead of full swims.

Sidehilling proved difficult at times, but gouged into most of the steep, rocky slopes were old trails used by not only caribou but also

Dall sheep. We spotted a few of the all-white animals running away—shorter and stockier figures than the ones we were used to following, but just as impressive, especially the heavily muscled males with their huge, curving horns. But the farther south we traveled, the less of anything we saw, for as we drew closer to tree line, the ankle-deep carpet of tundra became a head-high thicket of brush.

"This isn't walking, it's fighting," Leanne complained as we broke free of one valley and looked into the green and gold swirls of brush that lay ahead.

I nodded, wiping at a cheek where one of many scratches oozed blood. I wanted to say something encouraging but, after glassing the upper Bell River valley where we were headed, decided to stay quiet. The swales of vegetation there looked thicker and higher than anything we'd tackled yet.

They *were* thicker and higher, but the traveling became easier, not tougher, for the going had become so difficult that every animal before us had found itself funneled to the one and only path of least resistance, forming a tunnel of broken branches and trampled roots. Judging from the hair and hoofprints marking the path's woody walls and muddy floor, everything used it, including a shin-deep creek. I tried to imagine the majestic caribou bulls that seemed so at home on the tundra equally comfortable in the mass of stems and leaves, and I wondered how they negotiated their huge antlers around the tight and twisting corners that snagged and pulled at our packs.

The prospect of meeting caribou at such close quarters crossed our minds, but it was grizzlies that dominated our thoughts. Mixed with the caribou sign were tufts of crimped blond fur, berry-filled scats, and huge bear stomps dozens of steps long. We had seen such stomps on the tundra—ritualistic paths where bruin after bruin had walked in exactly the same place—but none were as impressive as these. Each huge paw print had been worn a foot deep into the moss, every toe pad and claw mark perfectly preserved. Intimidated, I pulled out our emergency whistle and blasted it every few minutes for the rest of the afternoon.

My blowing went quiet when we reached the first finger of trees. These weren't the spindly specimens I remembered from tree line on the ridges that spring. Tucked within the sheltered and nutrient-rich folds of the river valley, they were thick spruce and cottonwoods that spread into a canopy 30 feet high. Overcome with nostalgia, we stopped and listened to sounds we hadn't heard in a long time: the buzz of thrushes, the chirps of crossbills, the back-and-forth chatter of red squirrels, and, most welcome of all, the rustle of wind in the leaves.

> *August 26—Headwaters of Bell River, Yukon—*I run my hand over thick bark and let out a subconscious sigh. No matter what comes—rain, snow, sun, wind—I know these trees will shelter us. We are back in the forest, back where we grew up, back where heat and cold can be countered with shade and fire. My shoulders drop, and a wave of relief runs through me. After almost five months of exposure on the tundra, we are back where we know how to survive.

For the next two days, we followed the Bell and Little Bell rivers south to Summit Lake, seeing caribou where the forest opened into wet meadows, hearing them where it closed again, sounds that faded into the shadows in a staccato beat of snapping branches and tripping hooves. We too stumbled but kept moving, fixated on the two things that awaited us at the lake: more food and a borrowed canoe.

We'd been warned there might be hunters from Inuvik who had flown into Summit Lake, and when we turned the corner and broke out of the trees, the scene that greeted us confirmed the possibility. An orange tarp billowed in the breeze, and from a yellow tent came a man dressed in a brown wool sweater and camouflage pants.

"Good day," he said in a European accent.

"Hello." I looked toward his camp, then back at him. "Any luck so far?"

"Luck?" He paused, following my eyes to where a rifle sat against the tent. "Oh, you mean hunting! No, nothing for me, but the two others have gone looking." He sized up our loads. "And you? From where are you coming? You are hunting too?"

Leanne shook her head. "Not hunting. Following. We've been following the caribou for nearly five months."

"Ah yes! I heard of you. I am so happy we meet each other. I have many questions." He looked at our packs again. "But your rucksacks are heavy. We can talk after you make camp?"

Not long after our tent was set up, we heard the two other hunters descending the mountainside above, doubled over and grunting under heavy loads. There was no need to repeat my question when they walked into our camp: their smiling faces and bloodied hands already said what had happened. Although Leanne and I were weary and wet from a day of showers and rain-soaked bush, we did what is customary in such a situation: we introduced ourselves and offered to help haul their meat back to camp.

As soon as we saw the two slain bulls, we knew we'd made a mistake. Unlike the caribou we'd seen shot by Randall and James in the spring, these were now animals that we'd grown attached to, fellow journeyers we'd come to admire and respect. After defying the 50 percent odds of dying in their first year, they had gone on to survive the wolves, grizzly bears, river crossings, cold winters, and buggy summers that had tested them every one of the many arduous years since. Trying not to think of the injustice delivered by the bullets of two fly-in hunters, I swallowed hard and lowered a wrapped hindquarter into my pack.

The hunters—one from Inuvik, the other from Denmark—were good people, motivated not by trophies but by the satisfaction of procuring their own wild meat. But the way they talked told me they didn't really understand. And how could they? Like almost anyone else, what they saw before pulling the trigger was a single moment in a hidden life.

"They're real beauties, aren't they?" said the man from Inuvik.

I looked down at the velvet antlers.

"Fat, too!" added the Dane. "They must've had an easy summer!"

Leanne glared at him, then turned away, water gathering in her eyes.

"We'll catch up," I said as the hunters started off. "We'll see you back at camp."

The rain had stopped, and as the clouds lifted around us, the land that had been dormant all day suddenly came alive. Shafts of evening sun tracked from one side of the valley to the other, shimmering from peak to lake to peak again in great flashes of yellow and blue light.

"It's a beauty that can swallow you whole," said Leanne, watching as a rainbow took shape below.

I nodded, not knowing whether she meant the land or the caribou. It didn't matter—they are the same thing. Running a hand over what was left of one of the bulls, I searched for comfort in the textures, feeling the rubbery lips, the whiskered snout, the satiny cheeks we'd seen chew, snort, and cough so many times. Reaching for the upturned eye, I grasped the lashes with fingertips and gently pulled the eyelid closed.

"Leave it, Karst," said Leanne as it slid back up under my palm. "It wants to stay open."

News of our deteriorating condition must have spread around Inuvik, because when the plane arrived the next morning it came loaded with twice as many groceries as usual.

"It'll only take us a week to get to Old Crow, not four!" exclaimed Leanne as the pilot unloaded box after box of food. A little older and less hurried than the last one, he was game to banter for a few minutes before taking off.

"What are you complaining about?" he winked as he undid the ropes lashing the canoe to one of the pontoons. "I brought you a boat too, didn't I?"

"But are you going to help us carry it to the Little Bell River?" Leanne asked.

"Hey, I don't portage. I fly planes."

It took three carries to get all our gear, food, and the boat across the low, mile-long pass separating Summit Lake from the river—or, to be more accurate, two carries and a drag. We had neither the stamina nor the strength to lift the canoe, and after fashioning a set of harnesses from rope, we leaned into them like a couple of horses pulling a plow.

"Now we know why it's called the *Little* Bell River," said Leanne as we lowered the boat into the water: there wasn't even enough room in the narrow channel to turn the canoe around.

"Draw! Pry! Back-paddle!" I barked as soon as we were moving. The current was swift, the corners sharp, and around each bend was another slalom course of sweepers and half-submerged logs.

"This feels like the jungle, not the Arctic," I said as we whizzed past a blur of undercut banks and overhanging branches. Leanne nodded from the bow, pulling and pushing against the paddle, too occupied to look back. After an initial stressful hour on the water, the current eased off, a few more creeks poured in, and we began to relax.

The trip we had embarked on—a weeklong descent of the Little Bell, Big Bell, and Porcupine rivers to the community of Old Crow—is by no means difficult. Each year a handful of wilderness canoeists complete it, floating more than paddling down what is nothing more than a slow-moving lake. There are no rapids, no waterfalls, nothing to worry about except what's for dinner and where to pitch camp.

"Now this is more like it," said Leanne, leaning back on the gear and closing her eyes. The river widened, the branches parted, and we were flooded in sun. I stopped paddling too, daydreaming as we drifted effortlessly past a backdrop of bush, swamp, tussocks, and forest.

"It's great, but is it right?" I asked.

Leanne opened an eye and sighed. "Right? What could be more perfect than this?"

"It isn't exactly being caribou," I answered. "They're still walking. Isn't there at least a part of you that thinks we're cheating?"

She had heard enough.

"Heuer, are you kidding me? Have you already forgotten that we were starving just a couple of weeks ago? Have you forgotten how cold we were after the Blow River? Enough is enough. The trip is over. We did our best for four and a half months. All we're trying to do now is get back to Old Crow."

"Maybe you're right," I said, but inside knew I wasn't ready for where the river was taking us: toward hurry and disconnection; toward the things that had bothered us about the pilot and the hunters at Bonnet and Summit lakes. Being caribou had half-killed us, but simply going back to being human wasn't going to be satisfying.

As the river grew, so did the sandbars and beaches lining its shore, creating a brush-free corridor that pulled travelers out of the trees. It was mostly tracks we saw, but every once in a while we caught a glimpse of animals—a trio of caribou, a huge bull moose that dwarfed them, a lone grizzly floating with its head submerged, whooshing like a whale for its next breath. We drifted along as they walked and swam, following the riffle-pool-riffle cadence of the river as it shifted from bank to bank. Gold leaves from the birch and cottonwood trees rained down in the breeze, free-falling to the water that cradled them for a few minutes before pulling them under, carrying all of us out of the mountains and into the foothills in a twirling embrace.

Eating and dozing in the boat, we pulled off the river infrequently, doing so only to wait out a headwind or to camp. We wandered inland during those times, encountering more tracks and trails before the tangle of trees, swamps, and blowdown sent us trudging back to the tent. Sitting around the campfire, we listened to the geese fly overhead as the first stars in months came into view: waning days were giving way to waxing nights.

*September 3—Mouth of the Eagle River, Yukon—*Tonight I see I was wrong. Being on this river is just like being caribou, wandering across the landscape in a meandering, aesthetic line. This current has no keeper or master, no timeline to hurry it along. Carving its way through mud, clay, and mountains of rock, it moves with the kind of quiet strength and patience that impels pregnant cows past hungry wolves. It is gravity we feel, not thrumming, but its flow says the same thing: we will get there when we need to and in the way that is best.

The same morning a skin of ice greeted us on the shoreline, the Bell delivered us into the Porcupine River. Slicing through the turbulence, we pulled ashore at the confluence and climbed the hill to the same cabin where we'd spent the night with Randall and James exactly five months before.

"Well, this is it."

"This is it," repeated Leanne, drinking in the scene. There were no people around, only a padlock where none had been before and a pair of stuffed coveralls hanging off the porch to keep the bears away. A few dried pelts lay where the wind had pulled them off the porch, and I wondered whether any was the caribou skin Leanne had slept on the night she'd had that first dream. So much had happened since then, so many twists of fortune, and I tried to imagine what might have happened if we'd never met Randall. Would we still have circled with caribou from winter range to calving grounds and back? Would we have been standing here now?

"How does it feel?" I asked, sitting beside Leanne on the steps. A gust of wind set the scarecrow creaking, and a patch of dried flowers rattled in the cured grass at our feet.

"You mean coming back?"

I nodded.

She squinted upstream, staring at the gold trees reflecting off the water where thousands of caribou had stood on ice the spring before.

"I'm relieved," she smiled. "We pulled it off. I can't quite believe it worked out."

After a pensive moment, she turned and asked, "How about you?"

"Oh, there's relief," I assured her. "But some dread too. I'm not sure finishing the journey is going to be any easier than keeping going."

There were too many memories for the end to sneak up on us: the place where Randall and James had dropped us off; the slope where we'd followed our first caribou trail into the trees; the stretch of river where the hunt had happened; the spot where James had stopped the snowmobile and given me his speech about people, caribou, and jobs.

I didn't have any more answers or solutions now than I had back then, but I did have a truer sense of what was at stake. We had discovered a richness on the tundra that couldn't compare to money, a wealth that had nothing to do with material goods or high wages. While we'd been caught up in the swirl of blizzards, bears, and migrating animals, the only economy and freedom that had meant anything were the economy of movement and freedom of thought. Guided by forces and knowledge we'd never known existed, we had stumbled into a dimension that neither university education, religious teachings, nor anything else in our Western upbringing had taught.

It had taken a while, but for a few brief weeks we'd become caribou: content in our suffering, secure in our insecurity, fully exercising the wildness that had been buried within us all along.

These are all mysteries and beauties the Gwich'in medicine men, Inuvialuit shamans, and others had long ago discovered but, in the rush of technology and conveniences, are being forgotten, even in places like Old Crow. That, more than anything, was what I dreaded: that in another few days, the vortex of consumerism would sweep us back into the shallows of modern existence, and the parts of us that had become caribou would shrink and die.

We could have pushed on and reached Old Crow late that night, but it was a journey whose ending couldn't be rushed. Feeling as though we needed one last, quiet night to contemplate all that had happened, we pulled ashore a few miles from town and camped one last time. An hour after the tent was up and a pot of water was boiling, the drone of an engine came from upstream.

We knew who stood in the boat long before it beached beside us. Clad in the same bloodied coveralls and fur hat he had been wearing when we'd last seen him, it was Randall, leaning forward and gesturing madly at the driver to take him ashore, leaping off the bow the second it hit the beach. We ran together, drank in the sight of each other's faces, then hugged as a threesome, giggling so hard none of us could utter a word.

"It's good to see you," Randall finally said, wiping his eyes. "I thought about you all summer. I was crying when I left you on the ice that day. Worse than I am now."

"We thought a lot about you too," said Leanne. "And a lot about your advice."

Randall pushed back to stare at us, still laughing tears. I wanted to tell him everything—the dreams, how minutes had become hours, hours days, and how time had rushed in some valleys and pooled in others—but I couldn't find the words.

"It was like you said ..." I began, but no sooner had I started than Randall held up his hand for me to stop.

"I know," he nodded. "I can see it in your eyes."

That comment kept both Leanne and me quiet for a few seconds, and in the silence we all filed over to the fire.

"We got a moose," Randall continued, bending back a few willows so he and his brother-in-law could sit down. "Took us five days and a lot of searching, but we finally found one. A nice young bull." He gestured to the boat.

I looked to where four large hooves pointed past the plywood gunwales then back at his brother-in-law, who smiled.

"We've seen some small groups of caribou crossing the river over the last few days," said Leanne. "Are people hunting them?"

Both men nodded.

"The herd's been crossing for a few weeks now, but they're really scattered," said Randall. "The weather's still warm."

The wind blew from one direction then another, and everyone leaned back as the smoke swirled around us. When the coughing subsided, we sat quietly sipping tea as the river slipped past. There was so much I wanted to tell Randall, so much to share. The silence was unbearable.

"Those caribou took us to some special places," I began again, "places we'd never been."

Randall shot me another glance that said, "Quiet."

"It really is good to see you," he said instead, eyes switching back and forth between Leanne and me. "You both look so different."

Leanne fingered her long curls and I tugged at my bushy beard.

"No," he said, shushing our laughter. "I mean you're *different*." He stared at us, into us, through us.

Leanne and I looked at each other and smiled. In a sentence, Randall had allayed another of our deep fears about returning to civilization: the fear that no one would recognize the profound changes that had happened over the last five months. It was as though every cell inside our bodies had been repolarized, and yet we were still trapped in the same skin. The man who had sent us off with just the right words had welcomed us back in the same way.

"Well," said Randall after a few more minutes, rolling onto a knee and pushing up. "We better get going."

I followed him and his brother-in-law to the river, knowing that although putting our canoe in their big boat and getting a ride to town was feasible, that invitation wouldn't come. Without having to talk about it, they sensed our need for one last quiet night.

"Just think," Randall winked before climbing over the gunwales. "Tomorrow you'll have everything: hot shower, soft bed, satellite TV, all the food you can eat."

I searched his face to see if those were good or bad things, but all I saw was a mischievous grin. Randall had long since made peace with the juxtapositions of modern and traditional life and the contradictions that lie between.

The far-off howls of a wolf pack woke us in the morning, yipping as we stuffed the sleeping bag and rolled the tent for the last time. Winter was in the air, a hard frost coated everything, and after launching the canoe we spent the rest of the morning steering clear of the shadows in favor of the warm sun.

We heard the caribou before we saw them: charging into the river from the trees, thrashing across the shallows like wild salmon. Fumbling with cameras and binoculars, we finally dropped everything to pick up our paddles and raced for the opposite shore. With Old Crow only 3 miles away, we knew this would be the last caribou we would see, and after traveling with them for 1,000 miles, we needed more than a quick farewell.

There were seven of them—four cows and three calves—and we watched as their hooves splashed across the gravel, water climbing up their chests. The current was swift, but they held their position with the shoreline, angling into the river's moving mirror of gold birch trees, yellow-green willows, and puffy white clouds. Heads high and tails erect, they swam between worlds, prying apart one reflection only to have a different, more abstract version ripple in their wake.

The river was more than a quarter mile wide at this point, and it wasn't until the animals were halfway across that we could hear the sound of steady breaths match the gentle flare of nostrils. Strung nose to tail, the cows and calves showed no hint of panic. Buoyed by hollow fur and propelled by paddlelike hooves, they looked as unstoppable as when we'd seen them dashing across the same frozen, snowy river five months before. We knew the truth, though. Swimming the Porcupine River upstream and downstream of us were other groups of caribou, each with fewer calves than had left the calving grounds in the summer, as well as fewer cows than had left the winter range that spring. Behind every animal lay a string of suffering across the tundra, and beside it was our own thread, circling from hope to renewal and back again, winding past images of birth and death.

There was no transition when their hooves touched bottom. Swimming flowed into walking, and the shuddering caribou came ashore beside us, showering the muddy bank with diamonds of water and light. Nibbling a few plants, the lead cow waited as the others gathered behind her, then they all looked back at their namesake river, turned, and were gone.

Leanne and I waited once the animals disappeared, hoping more would swim across behind them, but after we sat a half hour, none did. It was finally time to end our five-month portion of their much longer journey, one that had been underway long before we arrived —and hopefully would continue long after we left. Stepping back into the canoe, we pushed off from the shore and let the current do what we didn't have the heart to do on our own. Drifting west while the animals continued south, the river pulled us away from caribou for the last time.

Whether we paddled the last few miles to Old Crow was now unimportant, so when a motorboat came to fetch us an hour later, we didn't think twice about accepting the ride. Pulling alongside us was the same Gwich'in elder I'd met and talked with on the steps of the tribal office the day I'd come to Old Crow more than a year before.

"There's a feast waiting for you back in town," he said, helping us haul our gear on board. "Lots of food and lots of people waiting to welcome you back."

We smiled, then busied ourselves tying on the canoe while he poured a jerry can of gas into the tank. When he was done, he fumbled with the key for a moment, then hesitated and sat down.

"It must've been a helluva trip," he said.

"It was," Leanne answered.

"And you must have seen interesting things."

We both smiled.

"And ..." His voice trailed off as he looked at me. "And you must have ..."

I remembered what he'd said, how I'd disbelieved it back then, and I nodded now as I looked back at him, hoping that he too could see it in our eyes: we had talked to caribou, and caribou had talked to us.

We all sat there in silence for a few minutes, savoring the quiet warmth.

"Well, people are waiting," he said, standing behind the steering wheel. "You guys ready?"

Leanne and I looked at each other, then nodded.

Smiling, he leaned on the throttle and catapulted us back to another world.

A cow grunts for her newborn to come to her, while more caribou behind her wait to give birth on the coastal plain of the endangered Arctic National Wildlife Refuge, Alaska, June 2003.

epilogue

Leanne and I stood mesmerized in the subway station as lines of commuters poured down the escalators and stairways in a flurry of feet and legs. A twinge of recognition ran through me—not of place but of movement—and then the reality of where I stood rushed back in: the background din of sirens and bumper-to-bumper traffic; the panhandlers and security guards watching our every step; the buzz of helicopters circling the grid of high-rise buildings twenty-four hours a day. Five days and seven airports had come and gone since we'd left Old Crow, and although our bodies were in America's capitol city, our spirits were somewhere far behind.

Our feelings of disconnection peaked when we walked off the train, crossed the park, and without even thinking found ourselves veering to a patch of bare dirt on our way to Capitol Hill. There were no hoofprints, of course—Washington, D.C., is more than 4,000 miles from the range of the Porcupine Caribou Herd—and for a moment I felt silly for looking. But the embarrassment soon passed, for when I flipped the situation back on itself, I realized it only balanced out what was equally if not more ridiculous about the state of affairs across the street. Seated in their whitewashed chambers, members of the U.S. Senate and Congress who had never seen a caribou would soon determine whether one of the wildest, freest herds in the world would live or die.

We'd known beforehand that going to Washington so soon after our trip would be a shock. Even Old Crow, with its six streets, sewer truck, and couple dozen pickups, had seemed overwhelming when we'd first arrived back, but the invitation from an Alaskan conservation group to lobby on behalf of the caribou was too good to resist. They would set up meetings for us with senators and members of Congress; they would pay for a hotel. All we had to do was get there—and shave and get a haircut along the way.

After five months of moving under our own power, it was strange to sit and be moved, touching down in Inuvik, Dawson City, Whitehorse, Calgary, Toronto, and finally Washington with little sense of what lay between. All we felt and knew about a place was what we gleaned from its airport, and the trend was more stress the farther south we went: more televisions flashing in the lobbies; more billboards over the baggage carousels; more people pacing the halls with hands-free microphones, gesticulating madly as they talked and shouted to people no one else could see. I tried to stay open, to absorb everything, but by the time we reached Washington, I sensed parts of me that had taken months to open while moving with the caribou were already beginning to close down. And they had to. Life in the modern technological world carries none of the subtleties of living with caribou. There's too much to absorb, too much for sharpened senses to do anything but go dormant if one wants to survive. The instinctual search for tracks the next morning would be the last wild act to run through my body for a very long time.

Leanne and I had few expectations when we walked up the marble steps and into the first of four meetings with senators and congressmen, but we were nonetheless disappointed when it was an aide who sat down with us instead of the decision maker himself.

"You've got five minutes," she explained, pointing to the full room where men in suits of all sizes and stripes waited their turn outside the door: the American Automakers Association, Focus on the Family, the National Rifle Association—we were just two more people in an endless stream of lobbyists she had to listen to as we championed yet another cause. Searching for the right words to put into the right sentences, Leanne and I did our best to give an overview of what we'd learned about caribou on our trip.

The aide looked interested at first; she even moved to write something down when we mentioned the skittish cows on the calving grounds, but soon her leg was going again, bobbing in time with the second hand on the clock. We tried everything to pull her back, telling her about the bugs and wolves in the hopes she might conclude the caribou already went through enough, but when it came to oil development, her mind was made up.

She pushed the small stack of photos back toward me and slid back her chair. "That sounds like a wonderful trip," she acknowledged, "but the bottom line for voters on this issue is cheap gas."

"Pardon me?" I asked, unsure I'd heard right.

"I know it sounds terrible," she apologized, "but it's true."

The initial shock of what she said had worn off by the time we emerged on the outside steps an hour later, and in its place was frustration and despair. None of the other aides we'd met with had been as blunt and forthright as she, but behind their doublespeak was the same message. I looked out at the lines of traffic crawling past, at the limousines idling in the parking lot, and concluded that if change was what we wanted, then we had to take a different tack.

"We need to work from the bottom up," I said to Leanne. "We need to mobilize the voters. We need these people to feel the pressure from the people who put them in office."

I waited for her answer, for some sort of agreement, but she was too busy wiping her eyes.

Throughout the process of writing this book, and while Leanne edited and codirected the award-winning film about the journey, we both wondered whether it was a eulogy we were producing or a successful call to action. Time will tell, I suppose, but unfortunately time is running out.

Shortly after being reelected in November 2004, Bush and his administration, along with a new majority of Republican senators, didn't wait long before embedding a prodrilling resolution for the Arctic National Wildlife Refuge in a proposed budget for the entire country. It is a sneaky, underhanded method of moving a controversial issue through the political process, but when it comes to oil, this government isn't known for playing fair. Now, as I write this epilogue in summer 2005, one crucial vote remains. Sometime this fall, after months of discussion and refinements, the Senate and House of Representatives are expected to vote on whether or not to adopt the entire budget. Political analysts think it will pass.

If it does it will be a huge blow to the caribou, the Gwich'in people, and all other life that depends on that critical swath of coastal plain, but the fight to conserve the calving grounds won't be over. New court cases will be filed; environmental assessments challenged; protests, rallies, and other forms of civil disobedience organized and carried out. And maybe they will buy the time needed for the much larger shift that's required for the caribou and everything else on this planet to survive: the shift away from overconsumption and our polluting, plundering use of petroleum through the adoption of other, cleaner, healthier sources of energy, such as solar, hydrogen, and wind.

A number of blueprints are emerging for how we can do this, plans to guide us beyond a few token windmills and hybrid electric-gas cars and back to local, rather than global, chains of supply and demand. Real Cost Accounting is one of them; the New Apollo Project is another—paths that have been laid out for us to follow if we can only stop long enough to see and hear what's really going on. Our clean air is disappearing, the very climate that supports us is changing, and the last of the world's big wildernesses—the reservoirs of knowledge and instinct that flicker inside all of us—are disappearing, all so we can save a few dollars on our next tank of gas.

And what about the thrumming? Since returning from our journey, I have read books on infrasonic communication among elephants, sifted through journal articles about whale song, and stumbled across human accounts of similar phenomena, as in the poetry of Rilke. But I have found nothing about caribou.

"Sounds like a perfect doctoral project to me," said an excited thirty-year veteran of caribou biology to whom I talked extensively after the trip. "If you're interested, give me a call here at the university."

I thought about it for a few days but never got back to him. Some things aren't meant to have the wildness and mystery strangled out of them. Some things are best left in mystery.

Some things just need to be left alone.

acknowledgments

This story could never have been told if it weren't for the people and organizations that supported us when *Being Caribou* was no more than an idea. Thanks to Glen Davis, Mountain Equipment Co-op's Environment Fund, John and Barbara Poole, the Luxton Historical Foundation, *Backpacker* magazine, the Gwich'in Renewable Resource Board, the National Film Board of Canada, Jackie Flanagan at *albertaviews* magazine, the Yukon Conservation Society, Betty-Anne Graves, Pat and Ian Cartwright, Derrick Thompson, Michael Vidricaire, John Dupuis, Tessy Bray, the Von Tiesenhausen family, Surelog Homes, and Switching Gear for their financial contributions. John Irvine at Arc'teryx outfitted us with Gore-Tex anoraks and pants, and Don Gardner and Joan Dunkley provided us with ski boots, custom-made insulated covers, inspiring stories, and truckloads of moral support.

Executing the trip wouldn't have been possible without the logistical support of everyone at the Parks Canada office in Inuvik, especially Park Warden Terry Skjonsberg, who set the tone for cooperation early on. Park Wardens Mervin Joe, Herbert Allen, Steve Travis, James McCormick, Christine Aikens, and J. P. Kors all helped shuttle food caches from warehouse to airport, and Superintendent Alan Fehr and Chief Park Warden Ron Larsen granted me leave from work so I could do the trip. Thanks to Heather Swystun and Ian MacDonald, also of Inuvik, for adding fresh treats to the food caches whenever possible, and to Walt and Merilyn Audi of Kaktovik for doing the same in Alaska. And thank you to biologists Dorothy Cooley and Martin Kienzler of the Yukon Department of Renewable Resources, whose hints came at critical junctures when we fell behind.

A very special thanks to our friend Joe Obad, who not only helped write press kits, prepare food caches, and design and build our portable solar charging system in the final days before we left but also was supportive during the difficult transition when we got back. His presence was surpassed by only my sister, Erica Heuer, and friend, Cameron Johnson, who not only assisted with preparations beforehand but continued to work on the website maintenance, media communications, photo distribution, and publicity during the trip—all tasks they continue to volunteer their time toward today.

Then there was the journey of putting the story into words. Thank you to Kris Fulsaas of The Mountaineers Books for her careful scrutiny of the manuscript; Dinah Forbes of McClelland & Stewart for her thorough editing; and Milkweed Editions for seeing the potential to reach a wider audience with this important paperback edition. Megan Williams at the office of the Vuntut Gwich'in First Nation offered her perspectives while Don Russell of the Canadian Wildlife Service graciously shared his caribou expertise. Thanks to Erica Heuer and Jill MacDonald for their insightful comments on an early draft of the manuscript, and to Mike McIvor, who, once again, pushed me to think and write further each time I thought I was done. And the writing didn't come without sacrifi ce from my family, most of which was borne by my wife, Leanne. Her patience and support were remarkable given the excessive demands of our new baby boy, Zev

Finally, my deepest gratitude goes out to the caribou. Thank you for sharing your story. I hope this book improves the chance of it continuing in ways that are wild and free.

further reading
and resources

Calef, George. *Caribou and the Barren Lands.* Willowdale, Ont.: Firefly
    Books with Canadian Arctic Resources Committee, 1981.

Gwich'in Renewable Resource Board. *Nanh' Kak Geenjit Gwich'in Ginjik
    (Gwich'in Words About the Land).* Inuvik, N.W.T.: Gwich'in
    Renewable Resource Board, 1997.

Madsen, Kirsten. *Project Caribou: An Educator's Guide to Wild Caribou
    of North America.* Whitehorse, Yuk. Terr.: Department of Re-
    newable Resources, Government of the Yukon, 2001.

McCarthy, T. "War Over Arctic Oil." *Time* magazine, Feb. 19, 2001:
    pp. 18–23.

National Research Council. *Cumulative Environmental Effects of Oil and
    Gas Activities on Alaska's North Slope.* Washington, D.C.: The
    National Academies Press, 2003.

Rilke, R. M. *Sonnets to Orpheus,* in *In Praise of Mortality.* Edited by A.
    Barrows and J. Macy. New York: Riverhead Books, 2005.

———. *Rilke's Book of Hours.* Edited by A. Barrows and J. Macy. New
    York: Riverhead Books, 1996.

Russell, D. E., A. M. Martell, and W. A. C. Nixon. "Range Ecology of the Porcupine Caribou Herd in Canada." *Rangifer,* Special Issue No. 8, 1993.

Russell, D. E., K. R. Whitten, R. Farnell, and D. van de Wetering. *Movements and Distribution of the Porcupine Caribou Herd, 1970–1990.* Technical Report Series No. 138. Whitehorse, Yuk.Terr.: Environment Canada, Canadian Wildlife Service, 1992.

Russell, D. E., and P. McNeil. *Summer Ecology of the Porcupine Caribou Herd.* Whitehorse, Yuk.Terr.: Porcupine Caribou Herd Management Board, 2002.

United States Geological Survey and United States Department of the Interior. *Arctic Refuge Coastal Plain Terrestrial Wildlife Research Summaries.* Biological Science Report USGS/BRD/BSR-2002-0001. Washington, D.C.: USGS and U.S. Department of the Interior, 2002.

Urquhart, D. *Status and Life History of the Porcupine Caribou Herd.* Whitehorse, Yuk. Terr.: Yukon Department of Renewable Resources, 1986.

about the author

A graduate of the University of Calgary, Karsten Heuer has worked as a wildlife biologist and park warden in the Madikwe Game Reserve in South Africa, in the Carpathian Mountains of Slovakia, in Banff and Jasper national parks in the Canadian Rockies, and in Canada's northern Yukon Territory. In 1998 and 1999, he walked from Yellowstone National Park, Wyoming, to Canada's Yukon Territory to highlight a proposal for a 1,900-mile-long system of wildlife corridors and core reserves (the Y2Y Conservation Initiative). Heuer was awarded the Wilburforce Conservation Leadership Award in 2003. Along with his wife and son, he divides his time between Dunster, British Columbia, and Canmore, Alberta. *Being Caribou* is his second book.

After charging ahead of the herd, Karsten watches for caribou to emerge along the Firth River, Yukon Territory. (photo by Leanne Allison)

More Nonfiction from Milkweed Editions

To order books or for more information,
contact Milkweed at (800) 520-6455
or visit our Web site (www.milkweed.org).

Postcards from Ed:
Dispatches and Salvos from
an American Iconoclast
Ed Abbey, Edited by David Petersen

Toward the Livable City
Edited by Emilie Buchwald

The Colors of Nature:
Culture, Identity, and the Natural World
Edited by Alison H. Deming
and Lauret E. Savoy

Boundary Waters: The Grace of the Wild
Paul Gruchow

Grass Roots: The Universe of Home
Paul Gruchow

Bird Songs of the Mesozoic:
A Day Hiker's Guide to the Nearby Wild
David Brendan Hopes

On the Ice
Gretchen Legler

Arctic Refuge: A Circle of Testimony
Compiled by Hank Lentfer
and Carolyn Servid

The Future of Nature:
Writing on a Human Ecology
from Orion Magazine
Selected and Introduced by Barry Lopez

Hope, Human and Wild:
True Stories of Living Lightly on the Earth
Bill McKibben

The Pine Island Paradox:
Making Connections
in a Disconnected World
Kathleen Dean Moore

The Barn at the End of the World:
The Apprenticeship of a Quaker,
Buddhist Shepherd
Mary Rose O'Reilley

The Love of Impermanent Things:
A Threshold Ecology
Mary Rose O'Reilley

North to Katahdin:
What Hikers Seek on the Trail
Eric Pinder

Ecology of a Cracker Childhood
Janisse Ray

Wild Card Quilt: The Ecology of Home
Janisse Ray

The Book of the Tongass
Edited by Carolyn Servid
and Donald Snow

The Wet Collection
Joni Tevis

Milkweed Editions

Founded in 1979, Milkweed Editions is one of the largest independent, nonprofit literary publishers in the United States. Milkweed publishes with the intention of making a humane impact on society, in the belief that good writing can transform the human heart and spirit. Within this mission, Milkweed publishes in four areas: fiction, nonfiction, poetry, and children's literature for middle-grade readers.

Join Us

Milkweed depends on the generosity of foundations and individuals like you, in addition to the sales of its books. In an increasingly consolidated and bottom-line-driven publishing world, your support allows us to select and publish books on the basis of their literary quality and the depth of their message. Please visit our Web site (www.milkweed.org) or contact us at (800) 520-6455 to learn more about our donor program.